Through a Therapist's Eyes

Advanced Praise for
Through A Therapist's Eyes

Be careful how the power centre of your emotions can derail your life . . . how you feel in this moment will pass. Author Chris Gazdik shows us how the battle of life is won in the mind. Authentic, real, compelling, tales from an author who is in the trenches with broken souls.

—**Tom Dutta**, CEO of KRE-AT People Development, #1 International bestselling author, TEDx speaker, movie and film producer

A delightful reminder that fear, anxiety, and worry will block the kindness, compassion, and generosity inside each of us. Christopher shows us how we can choose to release those positive traits and become the best version of ourselves.

—**Dan Miller**, *New York Times* bestselling author of *48 Days to the Work You Love* and host of "The 48 Days Podcast"

I've cohosted the Through a Therapist's Eyes Podcast with Chris for almost two years now and have learned so much from him during our conversations and interviews. He has deep insights on therapy and mental health, and now he's compiled all this knowledge in print. This book will show you the world and life through his eyes . . . Through a Therapist's Eyes.

—**Craig Graves**, Unbeatable Mind coach and co-host of "Through a Therapist's Eyes" podcast

Christopher Gazdik is a master therapist, inviting his readers to join him in the counseling room to meet his clients. Although they remain anonymous, their stories are compelling and demonstrate their immense courage to grow emotionally and work through and resolve the obstacles that have hindered their lives. Through a Therapist's Eyes can certainly be read in one sitting, but I suggest you read it one brief chapter at a time—as a daily meditation—and allow its truth to sink in.

—**John-Nelson B. Pope**, **Ph.D.**, **LCMHCS, NCC,**
associate professor of Counselor Education at
Montreat College

In *Through a Therapist's Eyes*, Chris Gazdik provides a unique insight into the psychological workings of the mind. His knowledge and experience shine through to help other counselors, caseworkers, or anyone else trying to understand how to recognize and deal with mental health issues. It is a wealth of information with great possibilities for practical application.

—**Jim Fatic, MBA,** executive director of
Northshore Disaster Recovery, Inc.

I thoroughly enjoyed this book and realized about halfway through that I had begun to use it as a reference guide. It is much more than just a one-time read. As my life situation changes, I've gone back to several chapters to re-read them, and each time gaining new insight. The author has done a great job making the chapters short, understandable, and easy to apply to whatever's happening in your life.

—Cindy Englert, MA, CDP, CADDCT,
Ombudsman program coordinator at Centralina
Area Agency on Aging

Christopher Gazdik's *Through a Therapist's Eyes* is a must-read for readers from all walks of life. Gazdik blends his vast experience as a mental health professional with an easy-to-understand writing style. He takes on the challenge of breaking down mental health issues that plague many of us every day and delivers paths to a more mindful approach to solving our issues. Although no book could replace a face-to-face visit with a professional, this book comes as close as possible to an insight into the mind of a professional, almost as if sitting in his office.

—Jeremy Beardsley, software professional

Chris Gazdik is certainly one of the forefront thought leaders in the therapy world, and his engaging style of communicating his thoughts and expertise will certainly assist anyone who picks up this book. Highly recommended!

—Matthew Hanks, CRS, GRI, ABR, Realtor®,
team captain of Hanks Realty Group

through a
THERAPIST'S EYES

Reunderstanding Emotions and Becoming Your Best Self

CHRISTOPHER A. GAZDIK, LCSW

NEW YORK

LONDON • NASHVILLE • MELBOURNE • VANCOUVER

Through a Therapist's Eyes

Reunderstanding Emotions and Becoming Your Best Self

Published in New York, New York, by Morgan James Publishing. Morgan James is a trademark of Morgan James, LLC. www.MorganJamesPublishing.com

ISBN 9781631951701 paperback
ISBN 9781631951718 eBook
Library of Congress Control Number: 2020937679

Cover Design by:
Megan Dillon
megan@creativeninjadesigns.com

Interior Design by:
Chris Treccani
www.3dogcreative.net

Morgan James is a proud partner of Habitat for Humanity Peninsula and Greater Williamsburg. Partners in building since 2006.

Get involved today! Visit
MorganJamesPublishing.com/giving-back

To the well over 2,500 clients I have experienced the distinct honor and privilege to work with through life's challenges, which amounts to well over 20,000 therapy sessions. Your enduring courage to discuss the tough issues life presents us all has given me the unique perspective I share in this project.

Contents

Acknowledgments

Successful projects or works of any kind often are not accomplished alone. This project has come together with the encouragement and help of many people. I am struck, even as I write this, how many individuals I want to include. In simpler terms, I like to think of this book as a compilation of many therapy moments, which have developed over the years as I worked with people of all ages, numerous creeds, both genders, and many cultures. To all of these people, as pointed out in the dedication, *thank you*.

First and foremost, to God, the creator of my understanding. Through Him all things are possible as it has been written.

Lisa, my wife of twenty-two years now. I have told you before and believe it still: I have learned the most about life from you directly, our marriage, and the experiences we have shared.

My two boys Aaron and Adam. Becoming a parent is quite possibly the most life transforming blessing.

All my immediate or extended family members who are my "roots." From birth to this moment, in one form or another, you have supported me and enabled me to do my life's work helping others.

Friends. The word friend means a lot to me. Over the years, whether we have lived under the same roof or in different states, we have shared countless moments. I acknowledge that life is limited without you.

My Mastermind Group. The supportive environment we share to grow together and critically examine the important aspects of life and business have had a tremendous impact on this project and my life.

My co-workers. Those at Metrolina Psychotherapy Associates and those I've worked with in the past . . . I have gleaned so much personally and professionally over the years of practice that it is not measurable.

My editor, Cortney, with help from Carol and Sarah. Cortney, your immediate and supportive effort in the editing phase of this project enabled the finished product to become what it is. Your encouragement pushed me to the finish line. "Lefted to me own grammar skills alone, this here project might not likedly be readable!"

My publisher, Morgan James Publishing. Thank you for giving my book a spine and trusting my expertise and ideas enough to share them with the world.

Introduction

What seems like many years ago now, I began doing therapy with people. Prior to practicing therapy, I had interacted with people in psych wards, mental health centers, residential facilities, and through a crisis hotline. Somewhere around 1997, I earned the right to be called a therapist. I am also a child of God, a son, a friend, a husband, a son-in-law, a brother-in-law, and a father—in that order. I would be remiss if I did not gratefully thank those I have had the honor to be with in these relationships. I am especially thankful to God and my wife, both from whom I have learned the most about life. I would suggest that life is a dichotomous journey of emotional horror and amazing pleasure. I have decided to share what I have learned over the years *through a therapist's eyes*.

When I ventured into West Virginia University—however many years ago—I had the simple desire to help others. I have chosen to do this throughout most of my career using the tool of therapy. As the years passed, I found myself giving the same recommendations and presenting the same concepts over and over. As the repetition progressed, I found creative ways to say them; ways that allowed others to understand the message better or receive it in an easier manner than when I had first started as a therapist. I realized other people—people outside my therapy practice—would benefit from hearing these thoughts as well, so I tried to remember what the heck I had said through the years. Well, as you can imagine, that didn't work out so great because, well, my memory tends to suck. So I did what I thought prudent: write the thoughts down. Soon after, a book project was born.

I am often asked to teach emotional skills to people, especially for anxiety, depression, marriage, divorce, parenting, and communication. The question becomes, "Which emotional skill shall we choose?" Here in this project, I have endeavored to list only a few. I find that often times people don't know "what to do" emotionally, and since there are so many different options, I suggest trying a few of these foundational emotional skills. Furthermore, you may choose to try a combination of skills. This book is written as a reference to read in pieces, one small section at a time, because there are so many emotional skills to tackle. Feel free to skip around and learn one thought at a time, one moment at a time, one step at a time. Reading cover to cover is an option, too, but I find my mind gets overwhelmed with new skills—so much so, I lose the last skill if I focus on the next one too quickly. Maybe that happens to you as well. I will provide examples of situations that produce extreme emotional states and describe what purpose those emotions can serve.

My desire is to develop a reference guide aligned with my religious perspective but available to anyone. I openly acknowledge my faith in Jesus as my personal Savior while respecting others who carry different beliefs than me. I am not a Christian therapist but rather a Christian who practices therapy. I have found consistency between my work, my knowledge as a therapist, and my understanding from Christian religious teachings. I accept those who practice other faith traditions or those who do not have any particular tradition at all. Wherever you might be in your personal journey (with or without a faith-based perspective), I believe the concepts and thoughts I have included here will be helpful to you.

I founded a company called Metrolina Psychotherapy Associates near Charlotte, North Carolina. The tagline for my company is, "Working with you to create emotional growth." That is the truth about what I do as simply as I can state it. I have had the honor of meeting over 5,000 individuals, in more than 15,000 therapy sessions. Countless incredible, emotional moments have happened in these sessions and in my work with people, and I cannot possibly share all my thoughts with mere words. I also cannot fully convey the honor I feel from having walked with these people through their personal challenges and stories. The people with whom I have met are as much to credit for the thoughts in this book, as I could not have created this alone. After engaging in even one moment of reading and learning from one thought outlined in this book, my hope is that you will experience emotional growth, one step at a time and continue on your own journey of emotional growth however you deem necessary.

LET'S LAUNCH!

Christopher A. Gazdik, LCSW

The Self

The Self is the most important—and probably the most difficult—part of life to deal with. The battle within the Self is what we all struggle with the most. I have heard others refer to something called the "human condition." Well, that is essentially a synonym for the struggle within. At the core of our struggles are feelings and emotions, which include a range of insecurities and perceptions. And man, are they powerful. They can be abundantly wonderful but also abundantly painful, and the Self can move back and forth from one moment and feeling to another.

Think of young love—an adolescent sitting under a tree with a rose, going back and forth, first believing his or her target of infatuation loves them back and tossing a petal to the ground, followed by another pedal toss in absolute fear that his or her young love. . .*loves them not* and thus despairs.

"She loves me, she loves me not."

"He loves me, he loves me not."

We battle with the insecurities that the young individual might have but revel in the feeling and the possibility of being in love.

Picture yourself driving alone down a country road. Your windows are down. Your favorite song whispers out from the radio. You feel at peace, content as you take in your surroundings and the quiet environment.

Then your peaceful state instantly changes. A series of blue lights appear in the rearview mirror and suddenly, *ka-wham* . . . adrenaline flows and you feel anything but peaceful. Even if the police car passes you by, it will likely take a bit of time to regain that calm and peaceful state you experienced before those blue lights appeared.

This is the way our bodies are supposed to work, so embrace it. Far too often, we resist our emotions and try to suppress them. We don't want to cope with them. Doing this tends to be a mistake. Our emotions help us problem-solve and understand what is going on around us. They are there to help us make decisions and most importantly, take action. Paying attention to them can also lead to a non-action, which in reality is an active choice.

Generally speaking for those who live a faith-based life, a healthy order of priorities is God first (or the religious figure you subscribe to), then Self. For non-religious people, the Self is at the top of the priority list. If we don't take care of Self first, we are not likely in a position to take care of others. This is especially true with parenting. When we place our kids in a higher, or the priority spot, we become completely drained of energy and can lose ourselves in the process. In the short-term, we may not notice the loss of Self, and it may take years for it to happen.

Loss of Self is a certainty when Self isn't a priority.

The same thing happens when we put our spouses first. Basically, other people will drain us even when they have the good intentions of "filling us up." This is because it is impossible to fill anyone else up.

Think of this "fill up" in the form of energy. To be full, your emotional tank (a term coined by Gary Chapman, PhD) needs to be at a "10," which is full. When you give to others, that number goes down. Theoretically speaking, I guess if the other person gives you one-tenth energy trade every time you give them one-tenth, it is even and you can keep your tank full and the energy is full of positive vibes (good energy).

Unfortunately, it is highly unlikely to have an even trade because others around us have their own interests. Not only that, but let's face it, at times humans tend to take energy away from others to fill their own tanks and have nothing to trade, let alone to give. I know my kids will take energy—in a tireless manner it seems. They are kids after all. Truth be told, I must admit with a small measure of shame, there are times when I am not as nice as I should be to my wife, so not only am I *not* filling her tank, but I'm also draining mine. It is unlikely that being kind to yourself and building energy, will result in simultaneously draining yourself. Interestingly, with most faith traditions, you might think of the Higher Power as being fully equipped and capable as the creator of energy, thus there is an endless supply; but certainly, no human being has that capability toward another.

People often do one of two things during difficult times: shut down or ramp up with a hyper attitude and emotion. The goal, however, is to have a steady mind and emotional toughness. Being emotional people (that would be all of us) can be tough. Whether we express these emotions or internalize them, we must deal with them. I define emotional toughness as having the ability to be fearless in taking inventory of our emotions, being aware of what our attitude and emotions are, and then staying in that state and working through those emotions rather than disregarding them. This is referred to as positive coping. Coping when times are tough is wicked hard, but it has been said (and I believe it to be true), that **you grow the most when you hurt the most.**

Think of crisis situations. What is the first thing a 911 operator tells us? The operator says something along the lines of, "Okay, Mr. Gazdik, I need you to remain calm." If we're not calm, we tend to be more impulsive. We can't hear or think about the wisest actions to take.

I want to share a moment I had when I felt proud of my son several years ago to demonstrate this lesson. My wife and I have a close friend, Julie, who was watching our kids for us while we were out of town. During that time,

Julie was driving down the highway to a baseball game with our kids, and a tire blew out. Panic quickly set in. My son, who was sitting in the back seat, had an automatic response that led me to believe he clearly incorporated my guidance through parenting him to have situational awareness! He remembered what I taught him about being calm when chaos happens around us, and told our friend (I believe in a strong voice), "Mrs. Julie, remain calm and keep your hands on the wheel."

Hearing this story was such a cool moment (once I realized everyone was okay). From time to time our family will refer back to this experience with humor. The lesson to remain calm under pressure had stuck with my son. When emotions hit us hard in crisis situations, try to recall my son's words, and you can do it as well—bring your emotion to a lower level by breathing, slowing down, sticking to it, and resolving the issue. This mini-struggle between panic and composure is just one of the battles we frequently have within ourselves.

When you become proficient in managing the battle within, it is indescribably rewarding. Life just seems easier when appropriate decision-making is enabled. It's easier to love one another, and giving to others is possible because there is so much more to give. Successfully managing this battle is referred to as being emotionally healthy.

When you are emotionally healthy, it doesn't mean you always feel good. That is highly unlikely. In fact, you might often feel bad. But when you feel bad and manage the emotional content, it *gets resolved*. Far too often, we live in emotional states where so much moving emotion remains unresolved, and we develop "baggage." Baggage drags us down and acts as a weight that sometimes seems too much to bear. Managing the emotion, on the other hand, leads to expressions of relief.

"Man, that is a weight off my shoulders."

We have all experienced those moments. When we have an insight about our personal patterns in life, or are able to resolve a problem with our spouse or with our boss at work even, we exclaim, "Wow, I feel so happy." Sometimes in my sessions with clients, they reach a point when a weight has been lifted and literally want to jump in the air because they are feeling so light of heart. I want to emotionally jump in the air with them. Think of a touchdown (for all those football fans out there). Have you ever seen the fans in the end zone after a big play? They stand and jump and cheer with glee. Life is like that. Another example for many of us may be when we see our child accomplish a major feat. We just can't help but to stand and yell out or cry with delight after they worked so hard to succeed. There are many examples where persevering through the battle within can become this rewarding.

What we experience in our mental health comes from two basic sources: a genetically-based, biological set of factors and social-emotional factors. This is the nature versus nurture debate from Psychology 101. The biological factors are numerous, and there are some we don't truly understand yet. So let's focus on the social and emotional factors, which some could say we don't fully understand, either. When I say we don't fully understand them, I mean human beings are such dynamic creatures with complex biological and emotional dynamics, so we've developed countless theories and models of therapy to try to help. Physical and social-emotional interactions (events and people) cause us to feel things. These are powerful emotions forming us.

The following entries are in no particular order but designed to give you the tools you need to live a life where you can cope with, work through, and manage emotions in a healthy way. Off we go . . .

Chapter 1

Fears are usually irrational.

Do: Validate your fears.
Don't: Believe fears are automatically valid.

Fear is a powerful emotion. It is often the single most disruptive force in life. The funny thing is, fear is most often based on irrational beliefs or falsehoods. We have great potential to lie to ourselves with fear-based feelings. Out of fear, we can make ourselves believe all sorts of things that are not true about ourselves, others, or the situations we face.

How many things are people afraid of? The fear of being alone, public speaking, flying, heights, the dark, death, failure, rejection, intimacy, and commitment are only a few fears on a never-ending list. Fear causes us to feel alone, in a state of consternation, and all twisted up inside. Fears of engulfment or abandonment, for instance, tear couples apart. (These fears, in particular, deserve another book on marriage . . . stay tuned.)

It might surprise you to hear these are all situations that can be quite enjoyable—even comforting. How can death can be comforting? Well, the loss of a loved one or of one's own life is scary, but on the other hand, Heaven is considered by many to be a pretty enjoyable place (for those who believe in the experience of Heaven). With such an experience of Heaven there is no further sorrow, suffering, or pain—emotional or physical. Once this ultimate outcome is embraced as a possibility, the fear is no longer in control and thus, we can successfully battle against it.

Battle your fears. Don't believe they are automatically your reality forever.

Anxiety and other emotions are just feelings (or a state of being) for a set amount of time. Make no mistake, fear has its place and can be helpful, even life-saving. You should be fearful of walking down a dark alley at two o'clock in the morning, alone, in an unsafe area. This fear will help you to be alert and hyper-aware of your surroundings.

Fear is a real feeling. But we want to avoid automatically thinking that whatever is causing the fear is valid or even real. For example, it is very possible the alley is not really a dark and dangerous backstreet but a quiet and tranquil environment, such that I find on night walks all the time.

Fearlessness can lead to reckless behavior and poor decisions. This is why we must validate our fears. What does it mean to validate fear? I mean we recognize the feeling. We take note of it. Some of us might take a breath and ponder it for a moment (or longer) and just let it be a real feeling. Merriam-Webster defines "validate" as "to recognize, establish, or illustrate the worthiness or legitimacy." Sometimes, we can do this alone, within ourselves; other times we may need help from others. Validation, especially when it comes from others, can be valuable because left to our own resources, we are very susceptible to falling into the trap of believing our fears rather than understanding the lies they tell us. When this happens, fear can be paralyzing. As Franklin D. Roosevelt said during his first inaugural address, "The only thing we have to fear is fear itself."

Chapter 2

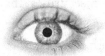

Insecurities can make us delusional.

Do: Challenge insecurities.
Don't: Listen to them.

Goodness, these crazy things called insecurities are a powerful force, and they often cause destruction. Either destruction of a moment, a situation, or even a whole person! Delusional, as defined by Dictionary.com, is "having false or unrealistic beliefs or opinions." False beliefs or unrealistic thinking patterns can develop suddenly or over a long period of time. Life can turn turbulent in a moment's notice or slowly put us in uncomfortable situations over increments of time. Due to these situations or relationships, we can develop thoughts, reactions, or beliefs that are not based on truth but rather fear, which we started to discuss in the section above. This environment is how insecurities are born and grow. When insecurities are created, they tend to stay until we challenge them. If we don't challenge them but let them fester and grow, we tend to develop various delusions.

Often, people don't know when this process is happening. I spend a lot of time in my work with men, women, and children creating an emotionally safe environment where a person might accomplish the goal of challenging the insecurities that have developed in their lives. Sometimes, I provide an alternative perspective they can accept. Other times, they find their own way through it. I would like to provide a word of caution here, though. The concept of working through delusions or long-standing insecurities yourself can be dangerous. In the words of many recovering alcoholics I have had the pleasure to help, "My crazy self got me here. What would make me think my crazy self will get me out." In other words, they say the definition of insanity is doing the same thing repeatedly and expecting a different result each time. If you have carried a delusional state, or an insecurity that affects your functioning, then what makes you think you can expect your own thoughts to dissolve them? The main point here is that it really takes another perspective (sometimes, a professional perspective) to get through these nasty things— these insecurities.

How then do we challenge insecurities? Well, the point has already been made that often it will include someone else in your life. Probably not just one other person, either. Often it takes multiple people speaking into you over time for you to accept an alternate belief. Have you ever heard the advice, "If several people are telling you the same thing then you probably need to listen?" This is very true. Positive new experiences are more healing and helpful in challenging insecurities. You do have choices. "Choose your friends wisely" is another good adage that applies here. Wise and safe friends or professional mental health professionals can change our viewpoints and diminish our delusional thinking.

If you endeavor to challenge insecurities on your own, writing down the fear and reviewing it at a later time when your framework of thinking is different, can be effective. We can gain perspective when we are not in a state of insecurity about a situation or event.

In order to challenge insecurities, we must have enough alternative, believable input to change our mindset. Our problems begin when we try to move on, going from day to day without changing what we're doing or thinking. Stop, slow down, meditate, ask for advice, and write the recommendations and new perspectives out . . . these are some of the means to change our delusional ways of thinking.

Chapter 3

Insecurities are a cancer to the human spirit.

Do: Recognize and resolve things
you are insecure about.
Don't: Ignore the power of doubt
in your mind.

This is an important concept to understand. Insecurities are often the cause of great levels of distress for people. They create scenarios where people become angry, critical of others, demanding, controlling, envious, down on themselves, entrenched in poor self-esteem, unable to make decisions, unable to take action, poor producers, depressed, anxious, and generally all around unhappy. Goodness, insecurities are terrible indeed.

Cancer is something that destroys from within. It's the same with insecurities. They destroy us from within. The most dangerous time with insecurities is when they are active, and believe it or not, we may not even be aware when they are!

Not being aware of insecurities leads to deep trouble and is the main point of this section. So, how can we become educated about something we are not even aware of? It is easiest to recognize them when they are active.

My suggestion is we pay attention to ourselves when something is going on around us that fosters a higher level of energy, particularly negative energy. We can recognize the negative energy when a conversation is happening or a decision is being made and these cause our adrenaline to start pumping, making it difficult for us to think. Some experience shakiness or nervousness and don't know what to do. This typically means something has triggered us, producing a memory that is likely some sort of insecurity or fear-based feeling. When this happens, it is crucial we recognize it, avoid blaming others, and call ourselves out. We can make mention of it to a trusted friend, family member, or even the person we are talking with during the trigger. Ironically, when this is done the insecurity flare-up is oftentimes diminished. Sometimes, taking the courageous action of being vulnerable eradicates the insecurity—poof! It's gone.

There are many other thoughts or actions we can use to manage or rid ourselves of our insecurities. Throughout this project, as I use information, quotes, and stories to speak truth into you, I hope and trust many of your insecurities will diminish. We know when insecurities are resolved when we are able to make decisions, have conversations, or handle stress without the elevated negative energy described above. Man, what a great feeling it is to handle something stressful while remaining grounded and clear-minded.

Far too often, we ignore the power of doubt in our minds. It is no wonder, then, we find ourselves constantly having the same pattern of anger, fears, and insecurities, which act as that cancer from within. It makes me sad to think about how often this is a part of the human experience. I urge us all to empower ourselves by executing the "do" part of this concept— recognize and resolve the insecurities we harbor. If we ignore them, they will grow stronger and interfere with our lives. If we choose to ignore our insecurities and refuse to recognize them, the result is a perpetual cycle through life with emotional cancer.

Chapter 4

Guilt, fear, and insecurities twist reality into negative thinking.

Do: Work with the present reality.
Don't: Play emotional twister.

Emotions and feelings are what we all have going on inside our minds and hearts. They relate to the experiences we have. Simply put, they can be either positive or negative, and gradients span between the polar points of positive and negative. The most neutral gradient might be the state of being unaware or ignorant of an emotion. Be careful here, because some might think that apathy (lack of interest, enthusiasm, or even concern) or full emotional numbness is neutral, but these feelings often lie on the negative side of the emotion continuum. These feelings might even be a sign of anger, hurt, or massive insecurities. In any case, guilt, fear, or insecurity trigger thoughts, which we can spin in our minds, causing us to be caught in a nasty state of emotional twister.

Quick point here: Thinking is an activity in which we use our frontal cortex. This is the reasoning part of our brain; however, research shows us that a different part of our brain works much more quickly (about **twelve** times faster). It's the part of our brain that triggers what most might identify as our "flight or fight" command center—the amygdala. When we examine the brain, we can identify trillions of neural connections from the amygdala to the frontal cortex but only tens of thousands of neural connections from the frontal cortex to the amygdala. (Please don't hold me to the exact number of neuron connections as this is up to scientists to accurately number.) This explains how the fear-based brain dominates our experiences, more than the way we think or the content of our thoughts. However, we can control, or at least influence, the way we think. We cannot control much of what our brain interprets as danger from the amygdala. The research on this topic is a bit unclear, as our level of science continues to examine the complex nature of how this works.

What does all this mean, and what are we to do? First, when finding ourselves in an emotionally charged situation, we need to work in the present to manage that situation and try to regulate our emotions. Many strategies exist to help us do this—it's what my craft and science of therapy are often about. Simply put, we have both behavioral and cognitive strategies we can use independently or in combination.

- Slow down when we get into an emotional situation.
- Don't be afraid to stop a conversation or delay a decision.
- Refrain from avoiding conversation or decision-making altogether.

- Breathe, meditate, or pray.
- Talk to a trusted friend.
- Take a walk.
- Recite a favorite quote or mantra.

I find when we get emotionally "worked up," we tend to lose our balance in this emotionally charged or elevated state. The present reality isn't usually as bad as we think, and it may not be as good as we think.

Let me use a sports analogy to demonstrate our ability to manage our emotions in the present moment. To remain calm in a chaotic moment is similar to when players are in the zone; the game slows down for them. I interpret this to mean they are regulating their emotions well, thus they are able to play on a whole different level of skill. They also say in the sports world we need to stop thinking about the game while playing and either act or react to the actions of others in the game. For instance, in boxing, a counter punch is destructive. The boxer who is receiving a punch will make a slight movement, then return a punch often with devastating outcomes. The counter puncher seems to have the ability to remain calm in the face of destruction and deliver a blow that turns the tide in the fight. The overall recommendation is: When able, we must slow the situation down *in our minds*.

Mental twister refers to the state in which we become confused or in a state of "paralysis due to analysis" (shut down). I recently stumbled upon a quote (with an unknown author) that hits this idea home: "Overthinking things ruins you. Ruins the situation, twists things around, makes you worry, and just makes everything much worse than it actually is."

When we stay in our own heads, mental twister becomes an easy game we play.

One of the most important things we can do to avoid this is to *get out of our own heads*. This usually requires a good friend, family support, or maybe a therapist or pastor who is courageous enough to give us good feedback from another perspective. This would require us to talk to them or write down our situation so they can review the information. Only then can these support people give us proper feedback. Conferring with God—or some other higher power perspective—can also be effective here. The higher power in our lives can eradicate this mental twister by influencing us to replace it with a prayer life. Meditation can also be effective. Meditation might be thought of as being in one's own head, but often it is designed to "reset" our thoughts and to help us be more present in the situations we find ourselves, rather than overthinking them.

Franklin D. Roosevelt said in his first inaugural address, "There is nothing to fear but fear itself." We certainly add guilt and various insecurities into the mix. These forces in life definitely have the ability to draw us off into this emotional game of twister. We can resist this by slowing things down and turning negative thoughts into positive solution-focused thinking when we find ourselves in turmoil. We can use some of these emotional skills I've listed to slow things down—counter punch, if you will—and turn the situation around to our advantage.

Chapter 5

Emotional Fact: We will cope with feelings productively or destructively.

Do: Be aware of what you are feeling.
Don't: Ignore feelings.

When I use the term "emotional fact," I simply mean there is little question about the statement. From my point of view, we will either be productive or destructive in how we cope with our feelings. When we have positive emotions, we are more prone to positive behavior and decisions. When we have negative emotions, we are more prone to negative ones.

Let's start with the understanding that we have active emotions during every moment of every day. This is another "emotional fact." Consider, for instance, our sleep time. Sometimes, we wake up from a bad dream feeling an immense measure of shock or fear. Or we might find ourselves awakened from a pleasant dream experience, thinking, "Man, I would love to return to that dreamy bliss!"

People who are interested in advertising their products are very aware that our emotions are always active. It's the reason advertising strategies slither into every corner of our society. Television ads, billboards, radio commercials, podcast messages, and even whole cable news platforms use our emotions to sell products and advertisements. Strangers still call us on our phones, even though we haven't been looking at anything specific. People are paid to take advantage of our emotions, even when we are unaware they are doing so.

It is essential to become aware of our emotional state so we can take charge of our surroundings and drive ourselves to make better decisions and engage in more positive behavior. I find more often than not, we are unaware of our feelings or what state we are in during any particular period of time. Who really walks around with constant awareness? Golly gee, I think I feel glee. I certainly don't. We walk around consumed with all the external stimuli we face. These might include looming deadlines, knowledge (or curiosity) about what the kids are destroying in another part of the house, or the things we know frustrated our spouses. If we ignore feelings, we are likely to fall prey to bad behavior when our emotional state is stressed.

Successful people often talk about their ability to know what they are feeling. They will take what is called an "emotional inventory." This simply refers to the ability people have to stop for a moment and realize what mood they are in. Our commute home from work, for instance, can be a restful time to relax and settle down or decompress from the day's work as we prepare for home life. People claim they don't take work home with them. Is that true? Most days when I get home, I immediately take off my work clothes and put on more comfortable clothes. It helps me with the transition. When I've had a particularly stressful day, I actually wash my hands, imagining myself washing away the stress I feel. These are just a couple of ideas that facilitate our ability to be aware and take small actions to address any negative emotions.

Though there are many ways for us to cope with emotions and many therapy modalities designed to help us, I offer up what I call the cornerstone of mental health—self-care. I define self-care as fun, relaxing, enjoyable activities we engage in to distance ourselves from stress. They are hobbies or choices, which aren't self-destructive or work-related. For example, I like to use the self-care activity of gardening to help me manage my emotions. The plowing and planting involved in setting up a garden with plants and vegetables is work to some. We don't want to work ourselves to death, but the activities of light weeding and harvesting the garden really help me to get away from the stresses of life.

> **You have mastered self-care when you take the opportunity to break from the day's stress and return to the stress when you're ready or able.**

The break may be five minutes or five weeks, free or cost five thousand dollars. It doesn't matter as long as you can reset your mind and recharge your energy.

My goal is for us to be more aware of what we are feeling, so we are enabled to deal productively with decisions and behavior. We don't want to walk around unaware of our feelings or act rashly when we're stressed.

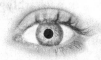

Chapter 6

Focus on encouragement from others or learn to encourage ourselves with positive thinking.

Do: Think "do" and act.
Don't: Think "can't" and stay stuck.

Norman Vincent Peale wrote a book, which was very influential to me in my youth, *The Power of Positive Thinking*. The title says it all. Earlier we discussed the problem with mental twister, which is devastating for sure; however, we need to recognize the choices we *do* have over our thoughts. We *do* have a God-given mechanism to help us control our thought-life—it's called our frontal cortex. It's the thinking part of our brains. When we focus on encouragement, we can accomplish incredible things. People say big things come from big ideas. Shoot, the grand idea I had to write this book series was nothing more than a thought about fifteen years before. Now it is actually happening. Negative thinking disables action. Here are a few negative thoughts I could have been stuck with if I had allowed them to hinder my progress:

- "No one would read the book."
- "The title is too corny."
- "I sucked at English class all my life."

- "I can't write."
- "I don't have enough experience."
- "People will criticize my thoughts if I put them out there."
- "I don't have enough time to spend on that project."

How far do you think I would have gone with this writing project if I had bought into this negative self-talk? The answer is not far. We must think, "Do," not "I can't," which is often followed with, "I don't."

My wife taught me the power of encouragement. On a cold day, wet from rain the day before, we rode our bikes with our young kids on the Virginia Creeper Trail. Travelling with two small kids is never easy. My wife hadn't ridden a bike in some time and was a touch unsteady. At the start of the ride, she swerved, and in a disastrous moment, found herself lying with her bike in a big, frigid, soaking, muddy hole. From a state of determined attitude, she mounted the bike to continue the ride but was clearly not thrilled. I felt horrible and helpless. There wasn't anything I could do to make things better for her. She picked up on this in some way and told me the simple truth, "Chris, all I need is a little encouragement." The simplicity caused me to feel incredibly stupid.

I thought, "Of course, that is what I can do . . . duh. Why didn't I think of that?"

One of the greatest gifts one can give another is encouragement.

I still fail at times in giving my wife encouragement, because I forget and lean toward the negative. I dislike that about myself and am still working to change for the better.

In a parenting relationship, encouragement is often the fuel our children need to strive (and persevere) toward their goals. I have an older brother who used to tear me apart when he criticized me, but oh my, in those rare moments when he was encouraging, I became emboldened to accomplish whatever feat lay before me. Have you ever heard the phrase, "Behind every good man, there is a good woman?" It may be a bit chauvinistic, but in any case, what do you think that woman is doing? You guessed it—encouraging!

A word of caution: Criticism can crush a person's drive. This tends to tear apart the seams of confidence, thus rendering the person disabled. Please don't do this to people. There are times when someone you know might need negative feedback when they are doing something that concerns you. This happens, for instance, (all the time) as a parent. There is a difference between positive criticism and negative criticism. The caution I refer to here depends on the nature of the encouragement. Without encouragement, criticism will definitely crush a person; however, with encouragement and feedback, they may be enabled to grow. The key is balancing correction with support and reassurance.

Encouragement can come from within—through positive self-talk—or externally from others. Craig is a friend of mine. In fact, he is the cohost on a podcast we currently do called . . . you guessed it, "Through a Therapist's Eyes." Craig often talks about "self talk." I know he uses this in his Jiu Jitsu training all the time. When he goes to a competition, for instance, his instructor has shared that it is very common to have a sense of fear or intimidation at that time. Craig's instructor points out the truth of the matter—the opponent most certainly has the same feelings of fear. Therefore, the emotional skills used in the competition include heavy doses of positive self-talk. Craig will go into a match with a truckload of self-affirmations he uses to feel more confident . . .

"I can do this,"

"I am a strong man,"

"I see this match as a challenge that I will overcome,"

"I will start strong,"

"I already won."

In addition, Craig's instructor is there for encouragement, as is the whole unit (team) that traveled to the competition together. It is a whole group of teammates encouraging one another. This is a great example of how we can execute positive self-talk and be the beneficiaries of external support from others at the same time.

No matter from where it comes, if we focus on it, give it, or receive it, we can do amazing things. I believe nothing is accomplished if we don't believe we can do it first. Encouragement breeds the belief "I can." Do you want to be in the NBA? Well, if you don't believe you can, you will certainly fail in that endeavor.

On occasion, you will hear professional or Olympic athletes call out that one person in their lives who said they couldn't do it, and that experience serves as a motiving catalyst. Michael Jordan shared with the world he was cut from his high school basketball team. I believe he was put on the junior varsity team for the 1978–1979 team, but in any case, this served as incredible self-motivating event for him. "Oh shoot . . . Oh, YES I CAN!"

But most times, people who have achieved great success talk about the people who believed in them, the ones who encouraged them, especially when they didn't believe in themselves. We can be intentional about surrounding ourselves with encouragers. And we can be an encourager to others. So off you go . . .

Chapter 7

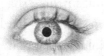

Depression can create a predisposition to negative thoughts but not a destination of negative thoughts.

Do: Think positively.
Don't: Allow yourself to remain
negative about things.

Depression hurts. That is the message the commercials we see on TV tell us. Well, it's true, and anyone who has suffered from depression can account for that reality. We need to clear something up real quick, though. Symptoms of depression are a bit of a universal experience, but having the diagnosable condition of depression is not. It is common for all humans to get sad or have a bad day. Those who have clinical depression have a far more difficult experience. They encounter intense feelings of hopelessness and helplessness, a lack of energy, zero motivation, and depressed interests. They are flat . . . despondent . . . and dark. We need to recognize this because when family members or friends try to offer friendly advice to those experiencing clinical depression—get out of your room, go do something fun, be active, or pick your head up—the depressed individual feels like he or she is at fault, because the typical things people do just don't seem to work.

For those who do have a depression condition, please understand these things people suggest do work in some cases, but for you, it is much harder because there are processes in your biological system working against you. Your serotonin and dopamine levels (neurotransmitters) have plummeted. I use the experience of grief and loss to help people understand clinical depression because grief and loss, which finds us all, mimics depression rather well. When we lose a loved one, we have very little appetite, can't sleep, and tears stream at seeming will. Things we know we are interested in just don't seem interesting any more, and most of life just doesn't seem right.

The following thoughts and recommendations are intended to help those of us who struggle with the state of mind we get into where people refer to themselves as "depressed," and not necessarily clinical depression.

Think positively! These are two words I hear tossed around often. It's a mantra people have used to write lengthy books. I mentioned Norman Vincent Peale and his work, *The Power of Positive Thinking*, earlier. Others have written of this too, so I will not spend a lot of time on it, but I hope we can all appreciate the real power in our thoughts.

I want to focus on the spot people can get stuck in negative thinking patterns, which is equally powerful— but in a negative way. When we remain trapped in negative thought patterns, we lead ourselves to a menacing place. Our perspectives on the people around us will shift, we'll see ourselves as bad, all of our situations will seem undesirable, and wherever we focus, life will be negative. When this happens, when we get stuck in this negative space, it can easily become our destination.

The suggested task, or recommendation, here is to switch this "destination" to a more favorable one. One example is rather than seeing the weeds in the garden, noticing the flowers you planted are blooming. We can choose to become more aware of the loved ones around us or focus on the friends who support us to find a destination that allows for a positive encounter, such as a shared smile. Things happen internally, physiologically, when a smile or hug is given or received.

When we are sad because negative things are happening, some of us have the predisposition to become conjoined to the negative circumstances and get down on ourselves, or the situation. We have the power to change this, though, so we do not toil there. We can choose a different direction and thus create a new destination. The destination we want to be in is one where we feel happy.

I will never suggest we turn a blind eye to negative things. We just need to be wary of making a negative situation a place of dwelling. When things look bad, we can ask ourselves this question: "What can I learn from this situation?"

Oftentimes, tough situations lead to the greatest growth. I remember being a young man in junior high when my family went through a divorce. This was an especially tough time in my life. My dad moved out, my mom went to work and to school, and later, my brother grew up and moved out. Suddenly, my whole world seemed turned upside-down in many ways. I had a hard time during adolescence, an already tough time for most teenagers. A depressed experience, looking back, could have held me down or sent me in a very different direction than what developed for me. Instead, I decided to focus on a different destination. I remember one particular moment in my junior high school. It was on the right side of the building, second flight of stairs, and exactly the second step. The thought hit me from nowhere. I was feeling particularly bad that day, but looked at the kid that was closest to me and realized that the person at some point has felt exactly like I did at some point in their life. Therefore, I immediately felt more connected to people and thus not alone. This was a powerful realization for me, which instantly helped me to have a different destination in being connected to others at a time when I felt people had left me to be alone.

Now don't get me wrong, recovering from these events in my life definitely took some time, and I made a lot of mistakes. I can now say, though, my emotional development moved forward in leaps and bounds. I talk about developing focal points in life. These are the aspects of life we choose to focus on. For instance, I remember developing this idea related to self esteem, which I still carry with me today—celebrate the things you like about yourself and change at least one of the things you don't like about yourself. The continued process, over time, means we celebrate more and more, and change one thing at a time more and more. The result is a Self we can certainly respect, right? When focal points are developed that target what can be changed, we experience a positive development in our lives.

Stop. Think. Develop an action plan that produces positive thoughts.

We need to develop our insight about negative places by finding the positive perspectives around us. When we choose to take action in this way, we will find ourselves in better circumstances from whence we came—a better destination!

Chapter 8

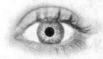

Happy people do good work.

Do: Deal with emotions, rest, and take action.
Don't: Neglect self and become unproductive.

We all want to be productive in what we do. When we feel unhappy, we might also be living in the space of "just trying to get by." I believe this is one of those "stuck spots" in which we can find ourselves. We have a responsibility to ourselves to work toward feeling happy. Happiness might come while we're at work, at home when we play, or when we're thinking. We all want to be good at something. Whether laying bricks, collecting garbage, creating companies, or playing sports, most of us want to excel at the things we spend most of our time doing. I love the song by Bobby McFerrin called "Don't Worry, Be Happy." This song says it all for this concept about happiness.

Employers need to be aware of happiness. So do parents, friends, and family members. Please refer to the prior section about focusing on encouragement; however, we need to make this a priority for ourselves. Far too often, people are guilty of not taking good care of themselves. In the section above titled, "Emotional Fact:

We will cope with feelings productively or destructively," I mentioned the cornerstone of mental health: self-care. When we neglect ourselves, it can leave us paralyzed, and we won't be good at what we do. How productive are we when we're tired, frustrated, or sad? People in recovery from alcoholism and various addictions have an acronym, HALT. It stands for don't allow yourself to become too *h*ungry, *a*ngry, *l*onely or *t*ired. We would all serve ourselves well to heed this advice, even if we don't struggle with addiction.

I heard an analogy I want to share. There are two people in a competition to cut as many trees down as possible in a twenty-four-hour period of time. One person decides to take a break on the hour, every hour; whereas, the other chooses to go at it as hard as he can for the whole time with no "wasted break time." Which one do you suppose would win? I put my money on the one who takes breaks. They might use the time to sharpen his axe or rest, thus enduring the physical challenge for a much longer time than his counterpart. Yes, the one who takes the consistent breaks wins, much like the tortoise that beat the hare.

A good question, born from this analogy, is, "What do I need to maximize what I can do today?" Maybe it's a "mental health day" to sharpen our axes, so to speak. Maybe it's an uplifting conversation with a trusted friend. It's different for each of us. The key is to figure out what works for us.

We need to be mindful of all that makes our minds and bodies work well so we can be happy. Nutrition, exercise, self-care, meditation, prayer, and good old-fashioned rest are the components of healthy lifestyles. I am concerned about our society and some of the patterns, which have developed. We are constantly "plugged in." This is why I have become quite fond of these treasures: nature hikes, avoiding Facebook, and working from home. Vacation is a time when we are supposed to recharge and forget about the world for a while. Too many of us tend to skip vacation or cheat our vacation time by staying at work. I am certainly guilty as charged on this one, for those who know me. Join me in working on finding a way to prioritize this.

I have learned so much from my wife about many things. Namely, to slow down, listen more, think a little longer before I speak, and avoid over-analyzing my thoughts. Through her own development, she has come to the conclusion she needs time away from others. We joke about a quote she found recently that says, "My alone time is for everyone's safety." For others, it may be that we need to be with others to recharge. We must understand what "does it for us." Most of us have heard and generally understand the differences between being introverted versus extroverted. Some feel drained by being in the company of others for any length of time (introverted), whereas, others get recharged by this (extroverted) and feel drained when alone. If we are not aware of how this works for us, then we are left with the danger of experiencing major energy depletion. It just will not work for people who feel drained when dealing with company to have company all the time.

In summary, we must understand what we need to be well—and thus happy—and then provide space for that in our lives. Neglect these things, and we will be unproductive, and eventually, unhappy.

Chapter 9

To give is good but to over-give can be destructive. It is nice to be nice, but is it better to be good to yourself.

Do: Give to others and do kind works.
Don't: Give more than you have to give.

This is a two quote special: two quotes, one message!

Me, myself, and I . . . three words in combination that may result in unfortunate avoidance of the need to take care of one's self. Selfishness is bad for our relational health and obviously should be avoided. I believe people can misunderstand selfishness, though. Merriam-Webster defines selfishness as "concerned excessively or exclusively with oneself; seeking or concentrating on one's own advantage, pleasure, or well-being without regard for others, or arising from concern with one's own welfare or advantage in disregard of others <a selfish act>."

The key here is the exclusivity of self, or not having regard for others. The truth is no one but ourselves has the responsibility to care for us. Even in parenting, the goal is to teach our children how to solve their own problems and be independent. A phrase made legendary after Laozi, the founder of Taoism first used it, "Don't give a man a fish, rather teach him to fish," applies here. The man needs to learn to fish to care for himself. Some people suggest we are in trouble when we look to the government to care for us, and there is likely truth in this. We can look to God to take care of us, but goodness, certainly not another human being, even if we are lucky enough to have a caring spouse.

Codependence is a significant factor here. I explain this in simplest terms as "being how another person is; if the other person is happy, then the codependent person is happy. If another person is sad or unwell, then the person who struggles with codependency is sad or unwell." The goal of a codependent individual is to make the other person happy so that we will be happy.

Some people go through extraneous efforts to please others in a codependent way. "People pleasing" is common. And there is a thread of codependent motives in this behavior. We all have interrelated relationships, but we need to avoid the codependence that exists in relation to others. Instead, we need to maintain our energy and care for ourselves.

Many people fall prey to codependent tendencies in parenting. Rather than working toward the goal of maintaining positive mental health, they become entrenched in their children's emotions, attitudes, and choices. I can't tell you how happy I am when my son hits a great ball during his baseball game or feels excitement over the prospect of a new job. Just today, as I write this, I have this news: My younger son learned he is first on the list for a new job. It will be his first experience with employment. I did not get him the job, but instead, he filled out the application, and I answered any questions he had along the way. I have to realize that if he doesn't present himself well, then I have to allow for the fact he might not get employed. I can give him some tips, and I did, but I needed to step aside, and let him succeed or fail of his own accord. This is hard to do when the stakes are high, as with older kids. But we have to remember to conserve our energy when dealing with our youth. They have to be allowed to succeed or, oh yes, fail on their own merit. We often desire to be selfless when we are caring for others, especially our children.

To be selfless is awesome for a time; however, if we maintain this for too long, we deplete our ability to be selfless again later.

We are not made with an infinite amount of energy, thus we need to recharge and maintain ourselves.

If we work too hard, we will feel drained. Give too much, and we will find ourselves empty. This is why religious leaders suggest turning to God to be filled up again. You might find you recharge best in nature, during meditation or prayer, or through a myriad of other environments or methods. The important factor is holding whatever it is that restores our sense of Self up as a priority in our lives. I believe God rested on the seventh day of creation, and my opinion is perhaps we should do the same.

In conclusion, let me also mention something about doing good works. The Boy Scouts have a slogan: "Do a good turn daily." This means do something nice daily, but not necessarily all day. Man, it feels good to help another. There are times we think we are helping the needy, but in reality, we find we are the ones who feel good on the inside. My son learned this recently when he engaged with the homeless during a youth group encounter. He was filled with a humble sense of Self, seeing people who don't have much but were grateful to receive what he was able to give. It brought me incredible joy to hear him describe how it felt to be kind to others. We can learn a lot through the eyes and words of fifteen-year-olds, but we need to teach them more about maintaining positive mental health. I encourage all of us to make this a priority, so we can *do a good turn daily.*

Chapter 10

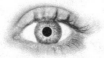

Why resolve feelings?

Do: Allow the process of
emotional development.
Don't: Ignore emotional developments
and create baggage.

There are very few things I would fight to convince others to think, accept, or do. I prefer to challenge people with different ideas and let them evaluate and grow in their own ways. This next particular idea, though, is one I do wish I had the ability to change people's minds about to convince them of its worth in their lives.

I want to persuade people to resolve their feelings. If we "let bygones be bygones," "agree to disagree," or let things be "water under the bridge," we allow emotions to remain unresolved. This choice comes back to bite us every time, and emotions have the tendency to bite hard.

Emotional development is a change in our level of insight or ability to express or manage emotions. It might also be called emotional growth. We don't want to simply move on from an event when there is an opportunity to develop a new perspective or understand things better. We want to grow.

In my practice, I have found people do want to resolve things, but often, they don't know how. So let me offer some encouragement. In each of our lives, we have been successful with resolving a feeling or emotion many times over. And it's quite a feat!

Consider a young teenager who is afraid his girlfriend doesn't truly care for him. When his girlfriend forgets to call him, insecurity surfaces, but with some positive self-talk, he becomes more secure again. He might suggest to himself, "Nah, man she just texted me earlier in the day that she loves me." Bam! In the teenager's own mind, he was able to resolve his own feelings. We don't always realize we are resolving feelings every day, but it is something we do constantly.

Many of the recommendations I offer in this project give guidance on how to accomplish this resolution process. Sometimes it does require something I myself struggle with greatly—patience. In time, if we remain vigilant and work through our emotions, the result of emotional freedom is well worth the time and effort.

First, let's define what a resolved feeling is so we know what the goal is. A feeling is unresolved if what we're feeling in regard to a person or event is as strong now as when the event or feeling first occurred. It is also likely unresolved if we don't have any awareness of how we feel toward a person or event, which is sometimes described as being numb. Resolved feelings are feelings we still have, but we harbor them with much less intensity. Let me also point out, we will find along the way of resolving emotions, the intensity of the emotion decreases gradually but consistently over time.

I believe it's true that a person often has the opportunity to learn the most or grow the most when they find themselves in the greatest amount of emotional pain. Religious leaders suggest this is part of the reason why God allows bad things to happen in this world. We can find this viewpoint in parenting, too. If I could protect my children from emotional pain and have them grow and learn things as well, then I would do that—no question—every time. The problem is, we learn from our mistakes and emotional pain can sharpen our character. When we work to resolve our emotions, we are growing! No pain, no gain, right?

To leave things unaddressed seems to be the easier choice. In the short run, it may well be, but in the long run, it creates "emotional (and subsequent physical) baggage." Unresolved feelings and emotions undermine our best efforts to be healthy individuals. Anger, resentment, shame, guilt, and so many other harmful traumas can last a lifetime without resolution or growth.

Allow me to provide an example. I had a conversation several years ago with a friend who described a situation that left me wondering about the issue of cost in not resolving our emotions. My friend experienced great pain for years following an event in high school where she was left waiting for a date that never showed. She was "stood up," as the expression goes. She was able to describe the situation with great detail, recalling the frustration she felt waiting for a few hours for the guy to pick her up . . . but he never did. For years, she held this against the young man, without any explanation of what had happened. She was not able to let go of it. It may have been helpful to focus on the possibility he was too insecure to face her, thus he made the choice to hide from her. This is a plausible explanation and one that allowed my friend to loosen her grip on the negative feelings she was harboring. In any case, he probably would not have made a great boyfriend or even date, and some might say she was better off not having had to deal with him.

Emotional freedom happens when we resolve our feelings. I would strongly urge you to make this a regular priority in your life.

Chapter 11

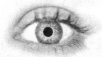

Accepting things is a part of your emotional growth.

I must give credit where credit is due, so to speak. This recommendation is not my quote, but rather my wife's quote. The following thoughts supporting this concept are mine. Lisa made this statement a while back, and it triggered an idea to include it in this book, because it is full of wisdom. It's spot on!

Do: Accept limitations, events, and characteristics.
Don't: Resist and fight against what is true.

Wise people cite three A's: Awareness. Acceptance. Action. This is a recipe for moving forward in life from those things with which we struggle. Let's initially tackle the first and third of the A's.

Awareness can be hard. The antithesis of awareness is denial, which can be easily misunderstood. Denial is not the rejection of truth, but rather an *inability* to see in ourselves that which is true. Alcoholics often struggle with denial. Someone who struggles with alcohol abuse is typically convinced he is not an alcoholic when those around him can clearly see the truth.

It happens to many of us in other ways as well. An individual might not realize he or she is a victim of sexual or emotional abuse even though they are living in an unsafe environment. People can be negatively affected by traumatic events, but when they encounter them regularly as part of their jobs or lives, they can become unaware of the chronic, harmful effects the trauma causes them.

So how do we create awareness and take action? Both are served well by listening to other people and the feedback they are brave enough to offer us. We often need an objective person, one who is outside of our own head, speaking truth to us to become aware of something. My wife has the ability to help me understand when I am emotional about something when I do not even realize it.

Regarding action . . . As with awareness, it might take an objective and trusted friend or partner to help us decide how and what action to take. If we develop our willingness to take action, we will find the appropriate action to take. If we struggle to know what to do, we can always ask people. Sometimes, many people. The more confident we become as we build validation about our actionable choices, the easier they are to take.

I saved the second A for last because I want to focus on acceptance the most. I believe it is the hardest of the three to gain. We are all fighters by nature, in one way or another. We are geared to fight to survive. Our brains are designed to diagnose a threat and the amygdala, the part of our brain that creates what you might recall as the "fight or flight system," gets triggered. This system is a primal and powerful part of our brains. It is the ultimate form of resistance. We're designed to fight and kill whatever the threat might be or flee in all haste if necessary.

Resistance is a part of our human experience and often can be good, but when we resist something that is true or factual—or emotionally factual—it does not serve us well. We must guard against telling ourselves, "Wow, that didn't just happen," or "I am not that type of person." Too many of us lie to ourselves. If it happened, it happened. If it is a part of you or your story, then it is a part of your experience. When we become aware of something about ourselves we don't like, we must work to accept it and take action to overcome it.

I remember an event I had as a teenager that many others have experienced too. I was driving home on a dangerous, ice-covered road. I was angry and hurt by a girl whom I learned was not interested in me. I had given her a necklace (I had found it earlier that night but I digress), and she gave me the "friendship speech." I was driving way too fast around a corner when I felt the car give way. In slow motion, I overcorrected the car, and it spun 360 degrees before it ramped backward down a steep bank. When the car came to a sudden stop, I sat there for what seemed like an hour as I listened to the song, which was playing on the radio. All I could think was, "That did *not* just happen."

Thankfully, the vehicle was not totaled, and I was safe, but obviously, I needed to accept that it did happen and get out of the car. I made it home that night via a kind stranger who gave me a ride. The next day, I went about doing the necessary tasks to resolve it with a tow and paying for a costly repair.

Successfully managing all three A's leads to the emotional growth we strive to achieve. We mustn't allow a lack of acceptance to stunt our emotional growth. As we become hostile or argumentative with our spouses, kids, family members, bosses, coworkers, and friends, it may be we are actually fighting the truth or ourselves. Fighting can be useful, but fighting against the truth is not. When we discover a problem, we must learn to stop. Simply stop and accept whatever it is. Accept anything, really. When we stay in our fighting stances, we are resolving to remain in denial. Resistance needs to stop.

Call things what they are. If you have been hurt by something, then accept the hurt and work to take action. If you have a painful event, don't lie to yourself and say it didn't happen. Guilt or shame results from denial, and people can live a lifetime carrying those burdens. If something is a certain way and we don't like, we can still accept it (and see if we can change it). Then, we'll be able to move on. Attempting to control things we really can't control leaves us feeling helpless and frustrated. We can sense when we've let go of some of our resistance because a certain calm seems to envelope us when the shock of the awareness fades away. Things may not sit easily, but when we do sit with them and acceptance is achieved, we can take action to work through the event and come to a conclusion. Acceptance can be the hardest of the three A's, but ultimately, it is the most rewarding.

Chapter 12

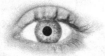

Some people falsely believe they don't have feelings or emotional experiences.

Do: Pay attention to emotions so
you feel them.
Don't: Put blinders on.

"I am just not an emotional person."

"Stuff doesn't bother me as much as it does you."

"Dang . . . that guy has ice in his veins!"

"I have never seen them upset."

"I'm not a sensitive person."

"I just let stuff roll off my back, man."

And my personal favorite, "I'm fine."

These are a handful of the thoughts and phrases that lead us to buy into a myth we want to believe is true. The myth that we don't have any emotional responses. We likely do this to feel protected from the feelings elicited from the painful crap in the world. This section could have been the introduction to *Through a Therapist's Eyes*, or at the very least, the first concept we tackled, because indeed, if we are to live as the emotional people we were designed to be, we have to dispel the myth that there are people who don't have feelings in the first place.

Simply stated, during every single moment of every single day we walk this great earth, emotion is—and will always be—part of the human experience. This includes during sleep. Have you ever woken up from a dream in fear or feeling freaked out at what you just dreamed? Or maybe you've woken from a particularly glorious dream had the thought, "Oh my goodness, please let me go back to sleep to get back to that dream!"

Oftentimes in my therapy practice, I come across people who don't know what they're feeling. This is simply because many of us don't walk around focusing on our emotions. Not many of us pause long enough to intentionally answer the question, "How am I feeling right now?" If we experience emotions all the time, then our feelings are changing from one moment to the next. This allows some of us to live on "autopilot" and we never pause to assess our changing feelings.

For fun, let me further complicate this. Is it possible to have more than one feeling at a time? If so, how many combinations of emotions might we feel at any given time? Goodness, when I find out about the destructive behaviors my kid engaged in during the day when I get home, I can instantly be flooded with various thoughts and feelings. I might actively wonder if I want to continue being a parent at all, or brainstorm what "parenting" methods I could get away with to avoid a DSS visit. (I love my kids dearly, just so you know.) When I calm down a bit, I might experience a flood of different things. Frustration. Fatigue. Possibly gratitude. Yes, often—and thankfully—there are many moments when I relish their growth through their apologies or attempts at reconciliation.

We can love intensely while being very upset with others, and sometimes these emotions toggle back and forth, from one moment to the next.

Don't confuse not knowing or understanding what you're feeling with not having any feelings at all.

Part of being an emotional person includes making emotional choices. Have you ever heard someone say, "Well you know, you are choosing to feel that way?" On a personal level, this comment drives me nuts because it is not entirely true. There is truth in this comment, but overall, it's not true. How?

You do feel the way you feel, but you can also make emotional choices to guide how you feel. The "Do" and "Don't" of this section tell us we can either focus on the emotion and feel the feeling or not focus on it, and not feel it—eventually. The emotion doesn't go anywhere. It gets buried, sometimes for a very long time; but without focus, you won't feel it in the present. You may not even know the emotion is still there, but I can assure you, it is very active within you. And pent-up, negative emotions create all kinds of problems, including resentment, hurt, and hang-ups. I want to encourage you to make a choice. Rather than walking around, being unaware of what is happening within ourselves emotionally, we can choose to understand the emotions we're experiencing.

Let's look at what I would call a bad choice in life. I call it "putting blinders on." By blinders, I mean ignoring the emotions we have, the ones we experience every minute. When I think of blinders, I think of horses. Now, I am not exactly a horse enthusiast, but to me, the blinders used in horse riding limit the information a horse receives. It helps them focus. We put them on a horse to make it more likely to do what we want it to do. In a sense, the riders become their eyes, and they respond to the directions and promptings those riders give them.

Human beings are not like horses in this way. We need all the information that is available. Limiting the attention we pay to our emotions limits the information our emotions are telling us, which in turn, limits the information we have to make emotionally informed, wise choices.

Now, let's think for just a moment on what to do with this choice we've just identified. Our focus does drive what we are aware of and also what we tend to feel. This is a bit of a simplification of emotion, but if you focus on the positives, then you will feel positively, and if you focus on the negatives, you will feel negatively. In life, we strive for a balanced ratio of positive to negative. Too much negative focus, and we'll hate what we used to love, and too much positive focus will leave us naïvely liking things we should probably distance ourselves from. I encourage everyone to avoid being the naïve fool that people make fun of, but to also avoid being that "Negative Nelly" people don't like being around.

Simply put, the goal is to achieve a balance of our focus . . . not too hot and not too cold. There is a time to focus and express what we don't like, but there is also a time to focus on and communicate what we do like. Make a choice, and choose wisely. Just please know, there is a choice to be made.

Chapter 13

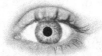

Expressed emotion is positive and fresh. Internalized emotion is stagnated emotion, often creating bad feelings, becoming "moldy or stale baggage."

Do: Express self.
Don't: Internalize things.

I like to depict the value of expressing emotions with a metaphor about water. Imagine two different bodies of water. The first has a water source where water flows in and water flows out. This might be a nice bubbling brook in the woods with a big pool. The water is clear and cool and highly inviting. The second body of water is different. The water has no source or mechanism of propulsion; the water is stagnated. Invariably, it will attract algae and bugs, grow murky, and become generally uninviting, especially for a swim. (It's the type of water an alligator would love.) Emotion is like these two bodies of water. When we keep things in our own heads, the emotion tends to get flat and the stagnation creates murky water, or murky emotion. It can become difficult to understand or make sense of our own emotions. When we allow ourselves to release our emotions, they can crystalize—becoming clearer, more manageable and productive.

Moving water is constantly filtered. I like ponds, so I have learned a little about how to create filtration for water. Novice pond builders often get frustrated trying to get the water to be clear. Well, that was me until my father-in-law (thanks, Jarrel) helped me understand how to make filters and effectively use rocks for filtration. Moving emotion is like this water. When we tell others of our emotion, they filter it for us. Have you ever been talking to a trusted friend, say something, watch their facial expression change, and feel something trigger inside of you? Perhaps you caught a glimpse of sanity after expressing a crazy idea or feeling you had. This happens to me all the time. Don't worry—you are not the only one who harbors irrational feelings. Let friends and family members filter these for you.

"Do express yourself, don't internalize things." I believe this is sage advice; however, I must mention, and I hope you understand, balance is necessary. It's possible to discuss our emotions too much.

Let's head back to the water metaphor again. Do you know what happens when water floods an area? If you had the opportunity to watch the flooding disaster left by Hurricane Katrina in 2015, you'll remember our collective hearts sank as we watched the floodwaters envelop whole cities. Typically, floods are devastating for people. They destroy houses, vehicles, and other properties. Businesses are forced to close and lives are at risk as bubbling brooks become dangerous, raging rapids, and whole cities are shut down. It's the same with our emotions, if we allow them to flow out of us without direction or control.

Religious leaders teach us, "Be slow to speak and quick to learn and receive, thus quick to listen." It's a paraphrase from the Bible. When we are too focused on emotional expression, we will miss this opportunity to hear or receive what trusted others offer us. When we achieve this balance of communication (but not over-expression), our internal work can be fruitful, but it is best processed when externalized. I would invite you to enjoy the feeling of "getting things off your chest" so you might become more clear minded and feel lighter in spirit.

Chapter 14

How do we handle stress? We feel what we focus on.

Do: Use a positive focal point
to deal with stress.
Don't: Dwell on that which hurts.

Stress management is a vast topic. Many of the ideas or quotes in this book, and in my practice, deal with this question of how we can handle stress well. A focal point is a thought or series of thoughts we choose to have in order to direct how we feel.

You may have heard the accusation, "You're choosing to be unhappy." Although this statement, in my opinion, is not completely accurate, it does carry a certain measure of truth. We don't choose how we feel, but we can choose what we focus on and thus, to an extent, how we feel.

When we encounter something stressful, there are multiple dynamics and unique characteristics within the situation. The stressor may be an event, a relationship problem, or a confusing or difficult decision we need to make. Each of these will have positive and negative, internal and external, and static and dynamic characteristics. If we find ourselves creating a focal point on those characteristics we can do nothing about and are not happy with, we might become bound to the desperate feelings of despair, hopelessness, or anger.

This happens frequently in parenting situations. I'll use the example of coming home from work (already feeling stressed) to find your child holding a note from school outlining his terrible, horrible, no good, very bad day. This might be a time to discipline your child, but while focusing solely on the opportunity to teach a life lesson, you stay angry and thus more prone to poor judgment.

Negative focal points do us no good and likely no good for those around us who have to cope with the negative outcomes of our choices. In addition, the negative focus— the despair-, hopelessness-, and anger-based discipline style—tends to hurt both the parent and the child. Instead, when we find ourselves in a place of stress, we can seek out that which is good in the stress, a bright spot, so we can cope with the stress better. When we find a positive focal point, such as the opportunity to help our children grow and learn in this case, we are more apt to feel better about getting through, or dare I say enjoying, the stress.

Did he actually suggest I might enjoy stress? Yes, enjoy stress. Look, life is stressful at times, even with things we choose . . . such as participation in marching band when I was in high school. I can't tell you how much effort learning to play a musical instrument involves. Many hours of practice goes into such a venture. Playing the trumpet for me began in the sixth grade and still in high school I was working hard to figure out this thing called rhythm. We began the school year a month and a half prior to students starting class in the hot days of August. Marching in the field of Wheeling Park High School we went to work learning the half-time show. It was painstakingly slow to learn each movement both in our marching and with the pieces our instructor chooses for us. Often times the kids would complain and seem to suffer under the hot sun and long days. We would go home utterly exhausted from the day feeling discouraged.

The payoff came for me especially during our show when we did what is called a "company front." This occurs when the entire band moves from a formation and dramatically forms a full line stretching almost all the way across the field. We would often begin playing our fight song, which would invariably cause the crowd to rise to their feet and cheer for us like the team just scored a winning touchdown. That feeling of a successful performance is quite a rush of excitement and ecstatic adrenaline. That feeling is certainly worth the stress and painstaking effort prior to even one such experience.

Another benefit of acquiring a positive focal point is the development of hope and confidence. Hope is a concept we tend to understand and value when we have it. I believe we can actually create hope within ourselves. When we examine which side of stress we focus on, we can choose the side that creates rather than destroys hope. The outcome of stress—whether it be a decision, situation, or problem—can be positive for sure. For instance, in the experience I described regarding the high school band, if I chose to focus on the hot days and long hours, not to mention the frustration I had with finding any sense of rhythm, then I might not have continued. Instead, I purposely focused on that one moment, at the end of the show on the football field, which I knew was coming. Hope manifests when we focus on the desired outcome and then focus on what needs to be done or decided to move toward that outcome. When successful, we build confidence, which empowers us to manage stress better the next time we encounter it. If we routinely use this pattern, we will find stress more than manageable. It might even be enjoyable.

Chapter 15

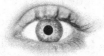

Life is too short to not be happy.

Do: Appreciate what you have.
Don't: Diminish or compare with others
the value of what you have.

I don't know who the Joneses are, but with a phrase like "keeping up with the Joneses," they must be some especially great folks. Of course, I say that with friendly sarcasm. The relentless attempts to acquire all the things we don't have or value to a high degree what other people have, are profoundly dangerous to our emotional health. Profoundly dangerous. We teach our kids this phrase about the Joneses to drive home this point. We've probably also used the phrase, "Son, would you jump off a bridge if your best friend jumped off a bridge?" I believe the messages behind these quotes are important for us adults, as well, because we tend to fall into the same emotional traps young people do.

So what do I mean by "profoundly dangerous?" Recently, I joined the masses inside the crazed world of Facebook. Now, I don't want to rail on Facebook, but I agree with my friend and colleague, Kelly, who calls this media tool, "Fakebook." People aren't necessarily fake when they post—and I would maintain I'm not fake when I post either—but let's face it, when I'm upset or otherwise emotional, the last thing I will do is post on Facebook.

"Ugh, my kids are so difficult to cope with!"

"OhhhhhMMMMMMMMMGGGGG . . . today at work, you will never guess what happened!"

"I am so stressed! My taxes came in."

Social media is a tool I use to keep up with those I care for personally to share fun times at the beach, let friends and family know about a nice award my kid received, or communicate my excitement about the sports I follow (like the Penguins winning two Stanley Cups in a row, YESSSS!).

However because of my profession and the subsequent insight, we can feel significant pain while watching what seems like everyone else's delightful life, in comparison to the hurt we might be experiencing. I must admit—I have become sad and envious at times when looking at some of the incredible things others are able to do that I don't have the opportunity to do. This can lead to feelings of depression. Sometimes, we find ourselves trying to manage high levels of envy, particularly when we are in an unhappy season in our own lives. I have often made the suggestion to clients they take a break from Facebook for this reason.

How you feel inside is the key to happiness. In therapy, we guide others on where to place their focal points, or perspectives. One way to change a focal point from comparing ourselves to the Joneses to one that leads to feeling better (happier) is to intentionally view the glass as half-full rather than half-empty. This doesn't mean we are lying to ourselves by changing the focal point from what we don't have, but it moves it to a place where we can appreciate the value of what we already do have. This leads to gratitude, which in turn, leads to a sense of happiness.

Happiness is a subjective sense of feeling good. It is an experience on the inside, not outside of us. Happiness is difficult to create with the wrong kind of focus. When we focus on things we don't have, we are doomed to a type of misery. When we rely on outside sources to make us happy on the inside—our spouses, kids, possessions, or money, we give up the emotional power to work on our inside, the true source of happiness. Faith traditions help us also look to God, or a higher power. This, too, is a way we target what's going on in the inside rather than external situations, objects, or people.

In the 1980s, Bobby McFerrin composed and sang the song, "Don't Worry, Be Happy." This is a simple concept that can create a significant measure of happiness inside. When someone is consumed with worry or sets out to change those things we cannot change (which we all have a strong tendency to do at some point), he or she is lead down the road marked with a great sense of hopelessness. Feeling happy is a purposeful action we take for ourselves.

Recently, my son cut the grass for the first time. I explained to him that when the task was finished, he might feel a sense of pride about his accomplishment for the rest of the week as he looks at the grass he mowed. The pride and sense of fulfillment that stems from hard work can lead us to feeling happy inside. Notice a trend. On the inside is where we can become empowered, grounded, satisfied, and sometimes a touch prideful, by what we *do*, and what we *do have*! This, as you might imagine, leads to feeling happy. In contrast, focus points on the outside of us that pinpoint what we don't have or what we are not able to do at the moment, lead to feelings of regret and perceived loss leads to feeling hopeless or less than.

So with those awesome lyrics, let's conclude this section: "Don't worry. Be happy."

Chapter 16

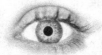

The value of working through life events is high.

Do: Be aware and move through life events.
Don't: Forget life events and
go forward blindly.

There are dangers in carrying "baggage" in our hearts or spirits. Baggage seems to be a well-known concept since we often hear people refer to it with statements such as, "I'm sorry for bringing my baggage into this new relationship," as in the cases of a second marriage or a second job after encountering some sort of unmanageable problem or "irreconcilable differences."

Unresolved thoughts, feelings, and life experiences detract from our current emotional health in many ways. They have been described as our hurts or hang-ups and develop into our habits. I heard a wise man (Ray, a friend of mine) describe a scenario where we are metaphorically connected to a wall with a bungee cord. We then try to "forget about it" and move forward (as in running forward or away from that which hurts us), the more tension the cord develops. It is an inevitable fact that the tension will become too great, and eventually, it will win out with the disastrous result of smacking us right back into the very wall we are running from (metaphorically speaking). In real life terms, it's not a pretty sight at all!

Many times in therapy, I work with people who are recovering from divorce. My current co-host on my podcast, "Through a Therapist's Eyes," said something that struck me recently. He suggested (after hearing this statistic himself) that it takes up to five years to recover from this type of life event. I have not heard this specific statistic, but I can say through professional experience, that if someone is starting a new relationship within that five-year period, I caution them to be aware of the patterns that were present in the first relationship, for without healing, they will most certainly be present in the next. Their main goal in a therapy experience becomes discerning these patterns and learning what to do to change them. Second marriages are sixty-seven percent likely to end in divorce. Without this awareness of the impact that life events have on us, we become blind to the emotional matters we face.

I find the most dangerous emotional matters that detract from our emotional health are those we are not even aware are there. Let's address this fact with several quotes. Focus, for a moment, on the logical question, "How can we be aware of that which we are not aware of?" It does seem daunting, but the answer is simple. The awareness needs to come from others. This is one of the reasons being a loner or being isolated from the feedback of others can be dangerous. We need friends in our lives that are willing and able to call us out on things. Or in better terms, help us see what we're incapable of seeing ourselves.

Professionals can also be quite helpful with this. We can receive coaching and guidance from pastors, rabbis, and other religious leaders. They can help us see, from a religious perspective, ways to be more aware of ourselves. Of course, God can be a huge guide in this endeavor if He is someone you turn to for growth and life-giving advice. Professional counselors or doctors are other good sources. Of course as a therapist, I would suggest therapy as the primary source, because it is designed specifically for this purpose, but really anyone with a caring attitude who wants what is best for you will suffice.

Even life experiences can be a source of awareness. I find that we learn the most when we are in the most pain, or in a dramatic life event. It often creates, by necessity, the willingness to explore emotional matters. This is why we need to move through them. When something is happening and we feel ourselves getting emotional, the natural thing to do is work to conceal or turn it off.

"Stop crying, man."

"Put on your big girl shorts."

This is a bad idea. I am not suggesting we stay stuck on things, but we must move through them. *Don't* work to turn off your emotions but rather learn to be aware, work through things, and avoid just moving on blindly. In any case, it is hard to forget the pain.

Chapter 17

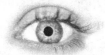

It's not easy to understand how to be a man or a woman.

Do: Find a good role model whom you value.
Don't: Guess how to be a man or woman based on cultural expectations.

"Be a man about it, dude." These are words men sometimes hear both as they grow up and once they become men. Men are told to be tougher, "grow a pair," or be stronger. In short, men are advised, "Don't be a girl."

My wife and I discuss that it's equally hard for a woman to know how to be a woman. They hear, "Don't be bossy, look pretty, don't eat that or you'll get fat, don't be a 'slut,' or don't be a prude."

We are fed so many different messages (good and bad) through culture, family, social media, and others about how to be a certain way. This can cause tremendous confusion for both genders, particularly when you look at gender norms. Men are supposed to be strong, but then are told to learn how to be a soft place to land. Women are supposed to be nurturing, but then are told to learn how to stand up for themselves. Our beings are comprised of our thoughts, feelings, choices, attitudes, and behaviors. How, then, are we supposed to figure out *how to be me?*

Without a role model (that you have chosen), we wind up guessing how we are supposed to act. Often, I believe people try to resist the "guidance" provided in the phrases above, which leaves us with uncertainty. Guessing how we are supposed to be leaves us open to two impossible options: know how to be yourself intuitively or meet all the expectations of others.

Poor self-esteem is born from either of these options. How can one feel good about oneself when met with the impossible goals we tend to set for ourselves? When we fail at balancing conflicting goals—be tough, be emotional—we simply cannot feel good as men or women. Likewise, we can't feel good when we feel like we're letting down those around us down.

As a starting point for finding a good role model, assess what traits you value in a person. Perhaps it's loyalty, honesty, persistence, being outspoken, or being quiet and a good listener. People have different characteristics, and they may all seem important. Prioritize them so you can choose someone in your life from whom you want to learn.

From early on, children have the ability to model behavior. This is done through something called observational learning. It's a survival mechanism. As we grow older, it is wise to choose someone to model for our emotional tendencies. A word of caution, though. Sometimes, we can model those who don't have the healthiest habits. Don't choose role models just because they are the popular choice or are in the public eye. Our personal relationships are more stable and honest. We know our parents, family members, and friends on a more intimate level. These are great sources for matching those things we value with traits of a person we know and thus learn from them. Watch them, talk with them, ask them questions, and allow their influence to mold you. This might seem scary, but if we choose wisely and find good sources, we can avoid the dangers of guessing how we're supposed to be—how to think, feel, and behave . . .

Chapter 18

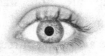

When we are the angriest, the more powerful "I statements" become.

Do: Make "I" statements.
Don't: Make "you" statements.

There is a common "therapeutic cliché," which says it is better to use "I" statements. Generally, this is true when working through something. In reality, though, when we get angry, we often turn more aggressive and blame others. The next step we take is to criticize others.

There are many forms of anger. No matter the trigger, when we're angry, we tend to look at others rather than ourselves. It is much easier to play the blame game, which deflects what we need to work through inside ourselves. Making "I" statements forces us to change our focus from that which others are doing to what *we* are doing. This leads to self-improvement.

On the other hand, making "you" statements is likened to using "fighting words." When others feel blamed for your feelings, it causes distress in your relationships. Now don't worry, this is a common event and you are in great company . . . we all tend to do it. This is because we have limited points of view that are highly prone to selfishness.

It's true. Human beings have limited perspectives. I like to think of it this way: when we speak, we can't even hear ourselves correctly. Have you ever listened to a recording of your voice? When I do, it sounds like I have a crazy pitch, like a cartoon character. On top of that, we hardly have the ability to see ourselves correctly. If we look in the mirror, we get a narrow perspective. We have to turn our bodies several different directions to see our whole selves. So if we can't see ourselves, hear ourselves, or fully experience ourselves, how can we really have a good perspective about ourselves? This is where selfishness comes in to play, because we worry about these things. It is the reason we can come off to others very differently than we intend. Consider the statements, "That's not what I meant," or "That came out wrong." It is important to our relationships that we be mindful about how and what comes out when we speak or act, given that we have the distinct challenge of not being fully aware of ourselves.

When we use "I" statements, we set up an examination process, so to speak. We ask ourselves, "Why am I so angry? What has gotten me so upset? What does this situation really mean to me? Do I feel angry or do I feel something else? Maybe hurt or scared, or overwhelmed, anxious, what do I feel, really?"

When we feel more intense anger, it's a signal for us to slow down and examine what the heck is going on, because more than likely, it is something internal. What can really lead to feeling so worked up in life as we can get rageful in an instant? Rage is a powerful and strong sense of anger that we can feel from time to time. Imagine for a moment, after a long and stressful day at work, coming home only to step on a pile or "nugget" of waste left from the family dog. The kids have stepped over this for three hours and refused to clean it up. As the parent, you certainly have the option—and often fall prey to the immediate impulse—to search out the kids and let the berating begin. Let's face it . . . kids do silly things like this—unfortunately often. It is a better option to slow things down, realize that work stress is likely fueling your rage, and avoid the option of any discipline in that moment.

The example above is actually one that happened between my brother and me. As children, we fought each other after finding the dog's waste in the bedroom we shared. Each of us refused to clean it up and several days later, it would be hardened! Goodness, this is hard to admit, but it's true. Sorry to out you brother! My parents never knew. This is a fact that we now can laugh about hysterically, but it might not have been that way if our parents had known this was happening. How enraged might they have become because of a silly decision we made as children? You owe it to yourself and those around you to become a more aware person in day-to-day life; many arguments will be avoided, and that is a good way to live!

So dooooo (get it?), make "I" statements. Spending a few minutes with "I" statements forces the process of awareness while "you" statements tend to create impulsive, rageful behavior that can do serious damage, especially in an accumulation of many small events.

Chapter 19

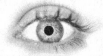

When you feel the urge to take action, do so. Dwelling on things tends to create anxiety.

Do: Act.
Don't: Dwell on things too long.

Have you ever heard of the condition "paralysis by analysis?" Of course, this is not a real physical ailment, but it is a humorous way to explain what happens when we think too much. Human beings have a super-developed part of the brain called our frontal cortex. This is the section that gives us the ability to think critically or problem solve. Our frontal cortex takes in many factors and extrapolates conclusions, given enough time to process them. We can ponder something for hours or even days. The problem is, we can spend too much time on this processing step, which is what people mean when they use the word paralysis. When we ponder too long without action or decision, we tend to overwork ourselves into worry, or in other words, we become anxious. May of us seem to love this state of pondering, as I have encountered a few people who have been settled into this "paralysis" condition for years.

Life is complicated. We need the ability to think and figure things out. This is one of the attributes that make us different from other species on this great earth. I find, though, some people are afraid to take action. We get hung up on getting it right (called perfectionism) or in making the correct decision. This can be a good thing, because we don't want to be the type of person who easily flies off the handle, so to speak. We call that impulsive. The trouble is we can't always "get it exactly right." Often times, there is no right answer. We must give ourselves a break. Some of us also need to give those around us a break and allow for mistakes and poor decisions. It's how we all learn and—hopefully—decide to make better decisions in the future.

Shoot, people are afraid of intended consequences. We tend to become highly worried or anxious about the effect we may have when we take action. When we take action, we may encounter unintended consequences. Often when we are thinking about an action to take, we are even anxious about what we intend as a consequence. In either case, the panic we feel if we are not careful can lead to no action at all or great levels of anxiety. I have met with numerous spouses who refuse to say things they need to say to their partner due to this fear of what may happen after they speak. Making no decision at all, can in rare times, be helpful, but usually, this is not a productive decision.

Think back to when you were dating. Do you recall the fear you faced when asked pointed questions, which trapped you into giving a specific answer? For example, nearly every guy I know has been asked, "How do I look in this dress (or any piece of clothing)?" Perhaps what you honestly think is, "That flower arrangement on the back of the dress looks like something out of the movie *Jumanji*." [This is a fictional movie where the characters are attacked by fast-growing, ugly vines that overtake the entire house.] In this instant, you're struck with fear. "What do I do now? I can't be honest. She will surely hate me." So it is a bit inevitable that what comes out is, "Yes dear, you look beautiful." Guys, you know I'm right. Obviously, this is a more superficial example of what are sometimes complicated scenarios. It makes it easier to study this issue with honesty. Other decisions, split-second or long-term, are far more convoluted.

When we apply this to those weightier circumstances, such as relationships with your in-laws, parenting choices, or complicated financial decisions, it's easy to see we can feel trapped and ponder our choices for years. Many of us arrive at the conclusion it is better to do nothing or say nothing than to make a decision or statement that will cause conflict. Because we cannot be certain the thought-process or decision is right or plan for all of the potential outcomes of our actions, doing and saying nothing seems to make sense. Then we become stuck. *Do* "act." *Don't* "dwell on things too long." We must make it okay— within ourselves and for others—to make mistakes and incur natural consequences.

When we've spent a little time being thoughtful and feel an urge to take action, then I am recommending we simply follow that urge and do it. Speak the opinions you have out loud, even if they are "controversial." The expression, "Say what you feel," means being open and honest. We can say what we feel when it comes to budgets, or boundaries with in-laws, or how to discipline the kids when they come home with a sword they bought online. (Yes, this actually happens.) We can always change direction if we need to or make a correction if it's warranted. **Taking action has much more potential for reaping a result that is desired; however, just dwelling on things often leave life's circumstances to chance that we will likely feel anxious about.**

Chapter 20

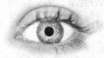

Humble people are happy people.

Do: Recognize and celebrate
what you have to offer.
Don't: Exhibit arrogance or
overestimate yourself.

Google says humble means, "having or showing a modest or low estimate of one's own importance." You want to feel happy, right? I contend humble people are happy people. Let's take a look at the flip side for a moment—arrogance, or overvaluing one's own importance. When you take the perspective of arrogance, you might feel important for a moment, but inevitably, you'll realize there is always someone smarter, faster, richer, stronger, prettier (whatever that really means), or any other characteristic you are focused on better than you. Of course, guys can't be pretty right? Handsome, I guess. The pressure to be superior ensues. There is an inherent burden in maintaining these characteristics, too.

I find as I age, it becomes harder to remain at my status quo. I can lose some weight, sure, but keep a hard, ripped body? Hardly. Shoot. Right now, those who know me would certainly say, "Chris, you have never had a hard body." (I am sure my wife and friends are losing it right now as they read this.) The moral of this story is we can—should—take some pressure off ourselves and avoid the arrogance we sometimes fall into. Similarly, we can fight the sense or thought of not measuring up to others. That type of negative self-belief is harmful too.

Feeling good about ourselves is a hard thing to do sometimes. The reasons are (as already mentioned) arrogance, self-consciousness, or being timid. When we compare ourselves to others, one of these reasons will rear its ugly head and prevent us from having a healthy perspective. When we compare ourselves to others, we fall on either side of the continuum of arrogance to self-consciousness. We must fight to keep ourselves in the middle—the sweet spot—which is being humble.

It is valid and important to recognize and celebrate what we have to offer. We should take note, and use our gifts and talents. I will always recommend sharing our great abilities with others. Nothing shared, nothing gained. I might suggest sharing a tasty dish you are good at making, or give a gift of an amazing painting you've created, or offer your knowledge on landscaping to improve a friend's home. I'm giving us all permission to celebrate our skills.

Go ahead, you likely deserve the recognition. It often takes years of dedicated work to become talented at something. Being humble doesn't mean not valuing what we have, or not celebrating our talents. So, yeah! *Do* celebrate you. *Don't* think you are better, try to be better than you are, or forget to be grateful for the skills you possess.

Chapter 21

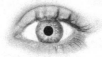

There is a need for balance between holding someone accountable while maintaining objectivity and not harboring resentment.

Do: Forgive others.
Don't: Harbor resentment.

Forgiveness is a tricky thing. When the lack of forgiveness becomes a clinical issue in my work as a therapist, I like to get a children's dictionary from my bookshelf and read the definition, which is simply, "to let go of anger against."

How many times when wronged by someone, do we hear, "Hey man, sorry about that." Then, almost flippantly, we respond, "Sure, no problem," then walk away angry. Understand forgiveness, in many situations, does not follow an apology. It is a separate and distinctly different step toward healing. You can forgive someone when they are not only not apologetic but also if they are disdainful toward you. Unresolved anger hurts us tremendously, not the person with whom we are angry. Shoot, many times the "offender" may not even know we are angry with them. In his or her mind, the painful event or words may be viewed with inconsequence, as if they never even happened. When angry, it is important to deal with this emotion and determine what action to take.

Have you ever heard the term "blind rage?" When we act through "blind rage," we're acting in an over-emotional way and become just that—blind. For instance, just two days ago, I watched my Pittsburg Steelers play a football game. If you follow this incredible franchise, you might recall the event that happened at the end of the game. It was quite controversial. A player from the Browns became incensed with the Steelers quarterback. He grabbed him and lifted him up off the field by his facemask and jerked his helmet right off his head. When a lineman tried to restrain him, the quarterback came back at the Browns player in anger, and the Browns player used the helmet as a weapon, swinging it at the quarterback and hitting him viciously in the head. In response, a different Steelers lineman ran at the Browns player with the bad intention of harming him—hitting and kicking him viciously. This all happened at the end of the game where it was quite obvious, with only five seconds left, that the Steelers were going to lose. In a hot minute, all of the players completely lost their minds and acted egregiously. In fact, the Steelers lineman who attacked in response admitted later that he "just blacked out." Talk about blind rage! These guys were completely out of control of themselves, had become blind with judgment, and they could have caused extremely serious injuries . . . seriously, if the quarterback had been hit with the crown of the helmet, he could have been killed.

When we are not filled with rage but "just" angry, we often say we have blurred vision. We cannot turn a blind eye, so to speak, when we are wronged. In relationships we try to use our best judgment. Judgment has gotten a bad rap these days. I often hear people being told they are too "judgy." Well, think about it, when you give a compliment, you are using your judgment. Having good vision in situations means having good judgment. When we become angry, our vision—or judgment—becomes clouded. We don't see things clearly. When we let go of anger, we can then let the other person know how we felt and what we see needs to happen. Look closely at how I just said that though. "How we felt" is in the past tense. Let go of anger so you can clearly see! This is why we must strike a balance with the forgiveness process.

There is a balance of holding someone accountable for their actions, but also having good judgment about them and the situation. When we let go of anger, we gain objectivity. In the above situation at the end of the football game, it could easily be said that the players were not acting objectively. In hindsight, most all of them regretted their actions. In a calm state, we can see the matter at hand more clearly.

In both my personal life and at work, I do not suggest people become doormats. Being passive is rarely the best option. People will overlook or take advantage of passive people. Neither is a good thing. For some reason, when we think about forgiveness, we mistakenly believe it's a passive action. It's not. I believe it could be the bravest choice we ever make. I invite you to see it this way as well. We must learn how to have a voice, but we need our voice to be shared from a position of objectivity, not out of anger. When we become angry, there is likely a problem of some sort. This "problem" needs attention. But be wary. The problem might be inside of *us*, so focusing on ourselves first is prudent.

If we are calm on the inside but still find the actions of others hurtful, then we can discuss things with them once we've achieved objectivity and forgiveness. With the ensuing interaction, problems can be solved. Who knows? Perhaps this is when we will receive an apology . . . *after* we were objective, let go of our anger, evaluated ourselves intently, and worked to hold the other accountable by using our voice to share how we *felt*.

Using this process, people can reach understanding and find peace. The relationship can thrive. The best part is we have peace inside ourselves. We cannot achieve this internal peace while holding resentment toward others. So *do* forgive, *don't* resent, and live in an internally peaceful state while holding other people accountable for their actions.

Chapter 22

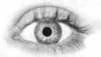

Grief: In regard to loss in our lives, we can logically plan for an event, but emotionally, it is still shocking.

Do: Grieve.
Don't: Delay grieving or avoid it altogether.

Everyone grieves in his or her own way. This is a common statement, and it's true. However, some ways are more productive than others.

Some people want to appear strong in the aftermath of loss, so they delay, conceal, suppress, over-compartmentalize, avoid, isolate, minimize, deny, or sometimes outright lie to others about their emotional condition in grief.

"I'm fine."

I do want to acknowledge it might be a good time to suppress, delay, or appear strong, as in situations when quick resolutions are required. For example, when a parent dies, and we are responsible for final arrangements or financial decisions. This is normal, but in the wake of all the activity, we must ensure we make space for the emotions to come out.

Look, this whole project is a bit of a guide on how to handle our emotions; therefore, I will not talk about this much in this particular section. When we are struck with a grief event, I see it as an opportunity—there is emotional permission—to be emotional. Embrace it because it is okay. I often hear from others that a funeral is the first place they've ever seen [so-and-so] cry or be emotional. This makes me sad in a way, because I believe we should allow ourselves to be emotional in many different life situations. In a weird way, I am grateful for grief events because they give us an opportunity for genuine expression in an environment that is granted social permission. For some reason, people feel it's more appropriate to be emotional at a funeral compared to other major life events, such as weddings, family reunions, long-awaited arrivals at the airport, tender moments at home with your spouse, or your child's first hit at his first baseball game.

Let's talk about the brain again. It can be said we have two parts: the logical and the emotional. When we contemplate an upcoming event, we often imagine what it will be like and how we will feel as we experience it. I went through this process as my super cool and remarkable dog named Magnum aged. He was my dog before I had a family. I met him in college and then found my wife and we had our kids. As Magnum grew older, I began to imagine life without him. I knew the reality that dogs don't live that long. It was a horrible thought, and it often made me sad, but I was largely logical about it. But goodness, I will never ever forget that ride to the vet's office with the decision to put him down weighing on me. He had come down with hip dysplasia, was whimpering in pain, had become incontinent, and was unable to stand up a few times. So we made the decision. During that car ride, as I tearfully explained to him, "I am here with you and will stay with you through this," my emotional self exploded. (Shoot, I have a tear in my eye at this moment reflecting on it.) It was as if I was shocked this was happening and was far removed from any of the previous logical thoughts I had had about this event for the past couple of years. My emotional experience took over. A different part of my brain was now active in this moment. Chemicals flow through our brains that enable us to cope or survive in immediately emotional situations. This is natural but needs to be managed, because unfortunately, we still have to make decisions, have conversations, and function when we are emotional. In my opinion, emotional decisions are generally not as secure or grounded as logical ones. This is the battle we face within ourselves when emotional events occur. When we allow emotions to take over, we are more likely to yell, act rashly, or be just plain irrational.

When we avoid emotional content, the pain actually grows even though we might feel better in the moment. This feel better condition is a lie and exactly what causes us to develop "baggage" as a result of the emotional events in our life. When we carry emotional baggage, we tend to experience the same feelings later in life, but they are exponentially stronger when we are forced to deal with them later. In essence, when we experience a new loss, we feel the feelings from that loss, plus the feelings from the original loss long ago, as well as any other losses we never processed.

I could offer a whole book on how to grieve, but here is a little secret: Grieving is nothing more than managing a set of emotions, ones which occur due to a loss in our life. Using the many strategies offered in this project is the answer to how to grieve a loss. Simply put, to grieve a loss event, you learn to manage the emotions you have rather than stuffing them down into your core. I offer condolences if you have experienced loss, and I urge you to become aware of your emotional self and manage the feelings rather than avoid them and create baggage. *Do* grieve. *Don't* avoid.

Chapter 23

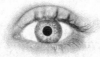

The body goes as the brain thinks.

Do: Manage your thoughts.
Don't: Ignore how you feel or think.

If you have read several different entries within this project, then you might hear a repetitive concept in the do's and don'ts: Do deal with yourself, and don't ignore yourself emotionally. "The body goes as the brain thinks," came to me during a client session one day. It is the concept that cognitive therapists have made their living on for many years. In my work as a therapist, I pull from the many theories and notions I have come across over the years, but the strategies based on Cognitive Behavioral Theory is one of the best places to start. Basically, therapists work with our negative thoughts to help us frame them in a different way so we achieve a balance with positive thoughts. The "body goes" specifically means the emotional experience we have plays out as the "brain thinks"—or as we perceive it will. This is really good news for us!

It is difficult to create an emotion or control our feelings. But it is easier, to an extent, to control our thoughts. At first glance, you might think it's a simple thing to do. Well, it isn't, and I'll explain why. Managing our thoughts is important because we are surrounded by automatic thought bubbles all day long, telling us how we should think and causing us to feel a certain way.

Thinking is another tool we use to manage how we feel. This is the good news. We can guide our feelings with this tool.

I'll use a sports metaphor to demonstrate this. In the game of basketball, the defender can be fooled if they watch the ball. The offensive player will make the decision to go left, but momentarily leave the ball on the right side of his or her body. In the words of my twelve-year-old son, this "breaks the ankles" of the defender by tricking them to move right followed by scrambling to chase down the offensive player who has moved left. So basketball defenders are taught to watch the waist of the offensive player because you cannot fake the direction your hips move. They simply go where the player is going. Our thoughts are like the basketball player's waist. Where our thoughts go is where we will go emotionally.

Our thoughts are indicators of how we feel. To identify how we feel, we can simply pay attention to what we are thinking. This is the process of thoughtfulness. Writing down our thoughts can be helpful because it helps to, what I call, crystalize them. By this, I mean it becomes clearer because we can read them back and reflect on them.

When we don't feel good about the thoughts we have, we can change them. We can focus on the positive aspects of any given experience, such as the things for which we are grateful, what we are learning through the experience, or how the experience might serve others. You might notice that the emotional experience is different; maybe more positive. Next focus on THESE thoughts and voilà! You have actually created a new emotional experience. Now focusing on the positive can be a hard thing to do when we are resentful or full of shame or guilt (which is a whole different issue). Even if we find these harmful beliefs shaping our thoughts, we can use truth and self-encouragement as allies in the battle against guilt and shame.

Facebook and social media are full of thoughts. We call them quotes or posts. Some of the posts highlight negative things, so we must choose wisely which ones we pay attention to, but motivation quotes are also prevalent. My personal favorites, which I have seen on Facebook, refer to the storms passing in our lives: "If you want to see the sunshine, you have to weather the storm," "Without rain nothing grows, learn to embrace the storms in your life," and my new favorite quote from Winston Churchill, "If you are walking through hell, then keep walking." Religious leaders will suggest memorizing scripture as a way to store away positive messages and thoughts. Good quotes or thoughts get us through tough times. We can use others' quotes when our own thoughts are failing us.

Chapter 24

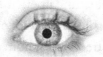

Boundaries are important markers between others and us. "With or without trepidation let others know where you stand."

Do: Set boundaries.
Don't: Avoid them.

Boundaries. People talk about them often. Sometimes, I believe it is our society's favorite "psychobabble" word. "What the heck are they anyway?" Looking to our good friend Google Merriam Webster, boundaries are "something that fixes a limit or extent," or elsewhere on Google, "a limit of a subject or sphere of activity." This sounds simple enough when we are talking about the boundaries of our property lines, but it becomes much more complicated in the whole relationship arena. Especially when that sphere includes people such as our kids, spouse, or those sometimes referred to as the "outlaws." For those of you who have delightful family relationships, that was a joke you many not appreciate. I am actually referring to "in-laws."

Boundaries are hard to create, maintain, change, or in many situations, simply respect. There are hundreds of books devoted to boundaries in relationships, and I would encourage you to explore them because boundaries truly are a challenging, but fundamental fabric of any healthy relationship. This section deals with only one factor related to boundaries—the trepidation humans seem to have with them.

"No, Dad."

"Sorry, Mom. We will be with my in-laws for Christmas this year."

"No, Sweetie, I am not going to do that for you (to your spouse)."

"No, Son, you can't live with us if you are going to do drugs."

"Hey man, you shouldn't be driving. I think you drank too much, I will not get in the car with you, buddy."

"I think you are wrong for having an affair, man (to your friend)."

Statements like these can be hard to say to someone we love or respect. Trepidation is a feeling we've all experienced—the feeling of needing to say something you don't want to verbalize. Holding our tongue is something we all must learn how to do, but saying what our limits are in tough situations is something we need to learn how to do also. And it can be tough to differentiate between the two situations. "Mind your own business," or "Stay in your lane," are expressions which can confuse the issue of setting boundaries. Sometimes we might not like what others have to say to us, but if we stop and realize it is likely very hard for that person to say it, we might catch the importance. We should strive to avoid being defensive, take what others say to us, and incorporate it into our decisions-making process. And in the reverse, if we feel the need to say these types of statements and set boundaries with others, we should do so despite the trepidation we feel.

Falling into the pattern of not giving voice to our limits clearly, or stating our opinions, will lead to internalized thoughts that might open the door for others to walk all over us, disrespect us (even mistakenly), or simply not know where we stand. It can also lead to resentment, failed relationships, or hurts that others don't even know we carry. Furthermore, others can learn from us, gain emotional growth through our courage, and respect us more for setting boundaries. When we become practiced at setting boundaries, our confidence and self-respect will grow, and we will engage with others better as parents, spouses, family members, and friends. So the "do and don't" of this entry is simple: *Do* set boundaries; *don't* avoid them in spite of any trepidation we experience.

Chapter 25

We are constantly a new or reconstituted self. We are not our "old self."

Do: Allow for change in self.
Don't: Be that old dog with no new tricks.

When I was a young boy, I watched my mom sit down with a jar of black olives and eat them. She ate all of them. I found this behavior to be most wretched. But guess what I love to heap on the top of my salads now? Tomatoes. Just kidding. Of course, it's black olives. This represents (in a small way) a change I've gone through. As time progresses, there are many things different about me now as compared to earlier in my life. I find myself in midlife, and goodness, it seems like everything around me is changing. I have the propensity to tear up if I think about the fact that I am no longer—and will never again—be the parent of an elementary, or even a middle school kid. Life throws things at us, so I know to be careful about saying "never." But the point is, life changes.

I want my "old Ronnie" back says a friend of mine named Becky. This is a common phrase, isn't it? Often, as in Becky's case, people are trying to convey they just don't like a recent development. Becky was struggling as she watched her husband Ronnie suffer with a heart condition, which had adversely affected his energy levels. Her statement was meant to convey she wanted him to be well again. On deeper examination of ourselves, though, how true it is that we pine for the days of old, or want to go back in time before something happened or changed. People tend to look back on their lives and wish they were younger. Some of us exult over our wedding pictures and wish we could go back to that time and enjoy getting married again. Some wish to be young and carefree with no kids, or go back to when we were actually good at sports, to when a family member was alive in this life with us, to when we actually had money to spend, or to our thirties, forties, fifties, or . . . on and on I could go.

Here is a life fact: stuff changes and changes again. Resist change and you will find yourself crazy with lament-laden thoughts and full of frustration. I hate change, like many others. I find it hard and scary—like a freaky-looking clown. But I realize the need to embrace it too. We are always developing new things about ourselves. We are always having new experiences. We need to always be learning.

My recommendation is *do* allow for change; *don't* be that old dog with no new tricks. I ask you to check out the next entry in this book, "Life is one big learning process with many opportunities to learn." These two sections pair together well. My goal is to shift the perceptions we have about change from "loss" to "gain," whatever the change might mean. For even in negative life events, we are able to encounter new life experiences, which can mean new lessons or new tricks in life. I know change can be hard, but it is a necessary function of life. If we allow ourselves to let life reveal things to us amidst the change, we can grow and develop these new tricks. I don't know about you, but I don't want to be an old dog with no new tricks.

Chapter 26

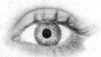

Life is one big learning process with many opportunities to learn.

Do: Remain open to things around you.
Don't: Close self off and remain dogmatic.

In the last entry, my wife suggested I had overused the "old dog" statements. Well, here is another "dog" reference—dogmatic. This word, as defined by Merriam Webster means, "characterized by or given to the expression of opinions very strongly or positively as if they were facts." When we are dogmatic, we tend to lose the open-mindedness that leads to growth. The quotable advice, "*Do* allow for change in self, and *don't* be that old dog with no new tricks" demonstrates just how much change happens in life. Life really is, as I see it, one big learning process.

As I think about the age-old question, *What is the purpose of life?* I have come to the notion that simply put, we are here to learn. We are here to learn healthy ways to live out our lives. Believers in religious circles might say striving to live in a healthier way leads us to "graduating" to a new existence when we pass on from this life. Is it that we live to learn so we might be more prepared when we die to enter Heaven? Well, I know I can never be good enough or learn enough to be given the entry to Heaven, but I can certainly try, and I want to be as prepared as I possibly can.

Whatever our religious credence, if we remain dogmatic, we will severely limit our ability to learn because we think we know the facts already. Let's not be that person. Instead, we should remain open to the things around us. In spite of dogma, this openness to change can reveal new and amazing ways of thinking or doing things.

I have learned so much as a parent. Watching my kids tackle their circumstances and choices, which I had gone through to some degree years before, has helped me learn in a much deeper way. I wonder, intently, how cool it must be for my parents and in-laws to watch my wife and me meander through the parenting adventures we face now. I hope they are learning from their experience as grandparents and parents as they witness all our screw-ups.

Openness doesn't mean you have no control over things around you or the decisions you need to make. We can't just sit back and let things happen with no influence and call that openness. This might lead to automatic or blind acceptance. We also can't just put ourselves in life experiences recklessly and call that openness. Opening ourselves to the wrong type of experiences might lead to difficult life lessons, even utter destruction. We do need to achieve balance and make the best decisions we can. So *do* allow and even make the decision to be in new experiences with balance, and *don't* remain closed off while trying helplessly to remain the same.

Chapter 27

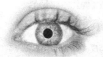

We experience most what we focus on the most.

Do: Focus on the positive aspects of life.
Don't: Drag yourself through all
the turmoil of life.

One day in session, "You experience most what you focus on the most" came to me in a fit of wisdom. We'll take a dive what I meant by it, but first, I have to admit I hate the phrase, "It is what it is." I believe it's used way too often. In essence, it means we are helpless to influence what is happening around us or decide what we focus on. We often feel helpless in life, especially when in distress, because life can seem so desperate and dark some days. I know people who've claimed, "I don't watch the news anymore." The news is not a true reflection of life, as the news media thrives on drama and the turmoil of life for ratings.

We hold the ability to exercise choice. We can watch the news incessantly and what will we experience? Anxiety. Hopelessness. Choosing to watch the news—murders, car wrecks, gas leaks, the criticism of expensive government programs, and more—(and believe everything we see is the totality of the news) will likely leave us with bad feelings about the world around us. Or we can watch birds in our backyard. Choosing to watch the birds—or engaging in any other positive activity—leaves us feeling relaxed and at ease with the world around us.

I do like sports, so please forgive me for another sports reference to demonstrate this point. Right now my favorite basketball team, the Los Angeles Lakers, is doing what is called in sports a "rebuild" of their team. They have been horrible for some time now after being one of the most storied franchises in the league, arguably for a long time. As I type this, the team's record is nine wins and fifteen losses. That is an awful winning percentage of .375, and puts the team among the bottom dwellers of the league. But there is hope for all Laker fans. We have a few young and new players who are showing promise, such as Lonzo Ball, Brandon Ingram, and Kyle Kuzma. So, I can make the choice to watch these young players who show promise and are steadily improving and experience *hope*, or I can focus on the rest of the team and experience *despair*, especially when I witness yet another loss or stare at the dismal record of nine and fifteen. In sports, there is a phrase filled with encouragement: "There is always next year." This is an example of focusing on the positive aspects of how the Lakers have acquired new talent and can help me make the choice to focus on the good aspects of life for the Lakers. I now have *hope*.

Not just coaches in sports, but all good leaders will recognize the good qualities within themselves, as well as what is good within the team. The leader on any sports team will search for the strongest player, such as Lonzo Ball, and build a team around him. This leader will highlight what

Lonzo does well on the court and add other pieces (player strengths) over time to accentuate what each of them can do well. Other leaders may search and find a strong piece of the team or method of function that works well and then focus on this strength to propel the team forward. This type of focus on the positive can yield great results and be sustaining for the future.

Interestingly, during the writing of this section, the big news that Lebron James had joined the Lakers had not yet happened. As a Laker fan, I have even more hope on top of the high hopes created with the team-building activities the Lakers were doing prior to the addition of Lebron. (See, things change all the time!)

Focusing on the positive, the good aspects of life doesn't mean we should be naïve and ignore the facts we need to pay attention to, but it allows us to give ourselves a break from negativity. We can appreciate what we do have, focus on what we value, and most importantly, learn what we can build on or improve. We must not drag ourselves through the turmoil in our jobs, within our family life, or among our finances. This leads to the type of despair we feel when things are not going well for us such as unemployment or divorce. We are not captive to our surroundings; instead, we are made captive by our own selves. We can be our own worst enemies. It's important to realize some of the horrible battles we wage emotionally are the ones within our own hearts and minds. What is your focal point? I invite you to change your focus so that you can directly change your experience.

Chapter 28

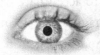

Taking things in small pieces and having small goals makes big things easier.

Do: Break things down—a lot.
Don't: Focus on the big picture when feeling stressed.

Breaking down big goals, tasks, decisions, or expectations into smaller parts is a very powerful emotion management strategy. There was a documentary on TV about the United States Navy's sea, air, and land teams, commonly abbreviated as the Navy SEALs—the U.S. Navy's primary special operations force and a component of the Naval Special Warfare Command.

Short side note: Thank you to all of our men and women in the military for what you do for us here stateside and around the world. Your service to our nation supports the very fabric of that which we all enjoy!

Though I am not an expert on any military facet, I did pay attention to the documentary, which discussed how the Navy improved their graduation rates. They focused on the specific emotion management skills, which successful candidates utilized, and shared how they teach these skills to candidates today. Incredibly, by doing so, the graduation rate increased from one-quarter to one-third. As you can imagine, few people make it through the whole rotation of drills and training because of the demanding nature of the program. One of these skill sets is a concept well known in therapy circles: "Taking things in small pieces and having small goals makes big things easy."

Using the SEALs as further examples, this concept is demonstrated in "Hell Week," a week of intense training the SEALs must literally survive. It is a time period filled with extremely challenging physical tasks that are designed to break the candidate down and make them want to quit. Most of these soldiers think they are not designed, nor do they have it in them, to quit. However, in "Hell Week," they often do. First, they run a mile and sit in the freezing ocean to the point of hypothermia, then carry boats down the beach, do a thousand pushups while instructors put sand in places sand should never go, if you know what I mean, followed by many other crazy and demanding tasks. They do all of this while limited to two hours of sleep and three minutes to devour each meal. Shoot, I try to think well of myself, but in reality, I would probably wouldn't make it past the first day!

In a review of the successful candidates, those who produced the documentary found the only thing they focused on throughout the week was one very small goal at a time. During the mile run, the candidates concentrated only on getting through that run. They might have been thinking, "I have done this a thousand times. One mile . . . no big deal!." When the mile was over, they celebrated their success internally. "The task is done, yeah!" Then, they transitioned to the cold water. Then, a thousand pushups with sand that burned their skin. They might find themselves getting through this so they can sit in the ocean and get cleaned off. When that task is over, they've achieved another success. Now they can celebrate by sitting in the ocean and getting cleaned off. When getting cold they might fantasize about a nice cup of hot soup they will get when they are able to get out of the ocean. It might take a while but they focus on the small fact that they will get out of the ocean at some point, and when they do, you betcha! They celebrate with a three-minute meal of hot soup.

Reflecting on the past five hours, they might experience great joy in the five successes they had. Then on and on and on it goes for a whole week. How far would they get if they focused on the whole week at one time while running a mile and again when doing a thousand pushups, all the while being yelled at, being criticized, and having sand thrown at them? That would probably feel like one long, impossible week to get through. Mindset matters.

I believe anyone can do this, not just the elite SEALs. We can execute these mini successes during any life task, right down to cleaning the house. It might feel daunting with three kids around. You parents know what I mean. Clothes, shoes, wrappers, food items, book bags, toys, sunglasses, and pencils seem to rain down from the sky, landing in every nook and cranny. They never seem to land in something called a drawer or garbage can.

Finances can be another example. Financial strategists often coach us to concentrate on the least of our debts and knock that one out first. When we do . . . you guessed it! We celebrate our success. This is often referred to as the debt snowball strategy—a guy named Dave Ramsey (a financial planner and budgeting guru) has made this sort of famous. If we focus on all our debt, on knocking out the five-hundred dollar credit card as well as the five-thousand dollar credit card, and the seven-hundred dollar student loan payment, and the four-hundred dollar car payment, then, well, the goal will feel daunting, to say the least. In summary, *do* break things down—a lot—and *don't* focus on the big picture when feeling stressed.

Chapter 29

Codependence: Fixing other people's problems so they will be okay, making you feel okay.

Do: Get out of the way so people can do what they need to do.
Don't: Stay in the way so other people will tell you why they can't do what they need to do.

"Codependence" is a clinical term, which has crept it into our society's "pop culture." Most people have heard of it and don't want to be called it, but often times, we fall into it—being codependent. I think it is important to understand what it really is from a therapeutic perspective so we can understand how it works in day-to-day life. Codependence is being what the other person is when it comes to emotional states. If the other person is well, then I am well. If the other person is not well, then I am not well. My behavior and efforts are directed at ensuring the other is well, so that I will be well.

This concept of codependence got its start in the 1960s and 1970s via the substance abuse field. We identified patterns within families that had an alcoholic or a drug addict. Clinicians saw spouses of addicts acting in peculiar ways. Spouses witnessed their addictive partners in trouble, and as an act of "love," rescued them from their consequences. Things like dumping alcohol down the drain, calling employers when they were too sick to make it to work, preventing them from driving when they drank, heavily monitoring their intake of alcohol, or making all kinds of excuses for their behavior to the kids and friends—lying for them. The list goes on.

The addicts' spouses felt miserable living a life where their partner was consumed by whatever drug of choice. Feeling so bad, they attempted to feel happier by making their partners happy, which unfortunately is impossible. Here is a little life tip: You will fail to feel happy when you try to make someone else happy. Happiness comes from inside; happiness does not come from the outside world or those around us.

Through anecdotal evidence in my therapy practice, I have seen codependence most often occur when a member of our family is struggling with a drug addiction. Parents of children who are addicts can easily fall into this type of dynamic. We work hard to make our kids happy and healthy rather than giving them what they need to take care of themselves—problem-solving skills and support. It can be tricky. Some of us mistakenly believe it's a parent's job to make the kid well; however, this type of codependent relationship brings a phrase to mind. "It is better to teach a man how to fish rather than give a man a fish."

In a parent-child relationship, it is easy to do our kids' homework instead of watching them struggle through it themselves. The child often gets "hip" to this and sucks us in to do it for them in the future. I remember a time when my oldest son was around the fifth grade. He had an art assignment that he was not motivated to complete. My wife, who has a unique artistic ability, decided to have some fun and complete the assignment for him. She points out to this day that he got an A+ for the assignment. I don't believe my son was even in the room when she completed the project. My wife recalls that he was in bed because he sprung it on her in the last minute. Ask yourself as a parent if you ever saw this particular universal skill—walking as slowly as possible to the task a parent is yelling at you to accomplish. Reminding a kid to brush his teeth is a common directive for a parent . . . this reminder is followed by that slow walk to the bathroom, which might include five more reminders before accomplishing the task. Here is a parent tip: The task only needs to be said once. We so easily fall into the trap of repeating ourselves many times over. This, to a small extent, is codependency.

I have created a continuum so to understand this phenomenon:

- Level One (neutral): Being connected to another person (having an acquaintance)
- Level Two (good): As a relationship grows we become interrelated (we care about and support or encourage the person—a spouse, child, or friend)
- Level Three (bad): Being codependent as described above
- Level Four (worst-case): Dependent (more severe forms of codependence)

This last level is highly destructive and draining. It is normal to be discouraged or upset when someone we know and care about is not well when we are interrelated. If our spouse, for instance, is upset, we can empathize with his or her and our mood will take a hit. We get into trouble, though, when we trip into codependence by trying to "make them well" ourselves. It can be hard to resist, but it's important to be responsible for our own mental health.

In order to assess where we stand within the four levels—related, interrelated, codependent and dependent—we can ask ourselves, "Am I trying to make this person well or am I just trying to help them help themselves?"

The do and don't become critical. *Do* get out of the way, and people will do what they need to do. *Don't* stay in the way so other people have the opportunity to tell you why they can't do what they need to do.

When a child we are responsible for, or a friend we care about, or a spouse makes excuses or creates bad focal points on why they can't do something they need to do, we need to get out of the way. The hardest thing to do is to back down or back away from someone you care about and let them struggle. It is very easy to step in and save them from themselves.

The stakes are high when their behavior becomes dangerous, as in addiction, for instance. The stakes often cannot be higher, sometimes life-threatening. No matter the level, the same concept applies. One of the most difficult challenges I deal with in therapy is working with a parent of an addict. Not allowing the child, at age twenty-something, to stay at home when they are active in their addiction means they may have to go live on the street. How do we get out of the way when they can be so destructive in their life? It is heart wrenching, to say the least. Often it takes professional help to discern the difference between "Am I hurting this kid by helping them with the basics of life?" and "Do I get out of the way and watch them struggle to the point of homelessness?" It is challenging and yet important to remain well when someone we are close to is not well. Take heart in the knowledge we often learn by the mistakes we make, even the destructive ones. We can learn to take care of self and thus recover . . . even from something as devastating addiction.

Chapter 30

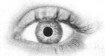

When our critical selves come out, it wears us out and wears others down.

Do: Accept self.
Don't: Expect others to fulfill us.

Happiness comes from the inside, not the outside world. For a moment, let's suppose what happens when unhappiness comes from the inside as well. We'll call this the "critical self."

We all have critical thoughts, but when they dominate our views for any length of time, it can wear us out! I have suggested hundreds of times to hundreds of people— especially teens— that we focus on three things we like about ourselves. Then, find one thing we don't like and make a plan to change it, always returning our focus to those things we do like about ourselves.

This process, replicated many times over, is what we call emotional maturity. When this process fails to develop for young adults and the critical self dominates our inner worlds, we will become overwhelmed, unhappy, negative, pessimistic, destructive, and impulsive. In essence, we feel "worn out."

The critical self does serve a purpose. Being critical of self is helpful for personal growth as long as it is not overused. When critical self-thought is overused or when we expose our criticism to others, it will not only wear us out but also those around us. No one likes to think poorly of themselves, and no one really enjoys hearing criticism from others. Praise is usually a better choice.

Praise is a powerful tool used to build others up. It works the same way as critical thinking inside us. Early on in my career, I learned from a gentleman named Shawn (I think I was actually still in school) to "sandwich a negative with two positives." With regard to relating to others, when we compliment people, they sit right up and feel good about themselves. It feels so powerful to receive affirmation, especially if we are hard on ourselves. Unfortunately, a really bad combination occurs when someone has an overactive critical self and receives criticism from an overly critical person. Then you have a double whammy. It might seem impossible for a person in this circumstance to feel positive.

The opposite of overly active, self-critical behavior can be harmful as well. If we focus too much on the positive, or exclude any negative feedback, we are naïve and out of touch with self.

The idea here is to focus on what we can control. *Do* accept self, and *don't* expect others to do that for you. People may give us compliments from time to time; however, they may also give us critical feedback. Shoot, others might flat out not like us. Relying on others is a bit unreliable as a way to feel fulfilled. We will encounter critical people, and if we allow that to "invade" what we think of ourselves, we become vulnerable to the "double whammy!" Critical feedback is helpful when it comes from trusted friends or family members who are willing to be helpful and give us this type of feedback out of love. Critical "invaders" typically have a different agenda, either self-promotion or competition.

We can use any feedback for our own development.

We don't have to be afraid of it, but we can't dwell on it either. I personally want my friends to help me in this way. There are many ways I can improve myself. I simply recognize this is a long process over the course of my life because I choose to focus on the things I like. Time is our friend here. When we receive constructive criticism, we should check it out with several other people to confirm it's valid. Then we can develop a plan to change it if we choose to do so.

But we can't forget to also focus on the three things we do like about self. Think about this for a moment. When the process you developed to change the one negative is executed, then you have four things positive to process. Wouldn't it be nice to have ten things we like coupled with one we don't?

Accepting self is a powerful way to live life. So *do* accept self and all the great things about you! *Don't* expect others to fill you; the best they can do is give you a compliment, which can be powerful, but not sustaining.

Chapter 31

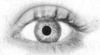

Focus on time. Flexible thought in the present is required to let go of regret from the past or worry about doom in the future.

Do: Stay mindful in the present.
Don't: Get stuck in the muck of the past or your dreams of the future.

Here's a little ditty that proves "every squirrel finds a nut."

Seems like ages ago when I was a child who had a super cool, original thought in my head. I was maybe eight years old. Sitting in my mom and dad's house, I found myself philosophizing about time. I know, right? What kid thinks deeply about time?

I thought then, and I continue to agree with myself now, our focus on time needs to be poised on the present, rather than the past or the future. If we focus only on the past, we miss the ability to make changes today based on the things we've learned. If we focus on the future, we miss the opportunity—in the present—to plan for or create the future we want. We can't forget the past or we would miss the opportunity to learn from it. We can't forget about the future so we have a vision of where we are going, but the point here is that it's most important to be mindful of the present.

The new component to this idea, which I added as an adult, is the need for flexibility. The present is the most important as it relates to time, but in the present, if we don't have flexibility, we will limit what we can actually do. Letting go is one of the hardest things I have found we can do emotionally—and describing how to let go is almost as difficult. Flexibility is needed for letting go. Dreaming of the future without creating action plans in the present is incomplete. Dreams are nice, but without action, they remain dreams. We need flexibility to execute a plan for the dream to become reality.

Regrets and fear of future doom will mire a person in a serious stuck point. Living emotionally free is the goal, being free from regret, fear, hopelessness, helplessness, doubt, shame, guilt, and other emotional states. Flexible thinking allows us to accomplish this.

By flexible thought, I am referring to the expression, "There are many ways to skin a cat." If we don't understand there are many outcomes to a decision we made in the past, then we will lack the capacity to let go of a bad one and lose the regret. If we don't know there are many things we might go through in the future that are not bad, then we lack the capacity to let ourselves execute a dream.

Let's give ourselves a break, I would say. Let go of bad decisions and let go of the doom we feel as we fear for the future.

"Let it fly."

"Let it all hang out."

"Leave it on the field."

"Live a little."

"Live and let live."

There is a theme here. Flexible thinking in the present is required to let go of regret from the past or fears of the future. So live free from the past and make the dream you have happen.

Chapter 32

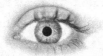

We choose what to focus on. What we focus on, in part, determines how we feel.

Do: Focus on realistic positives.
Don't: Focus on negatives.

Maybe you've heard of a guy named Jean Piaget. In Psych 101, we learned of this Frenchman who was the first to study how we humans think. He studied children in the 1930s to determine how our thinking process develops. Using his work as a starting point, several people have added to his thoughts to create what we call today Cognitive Theory. Many therapists operate from an offshoot of this theory, which combines the ideas and strategies with Behavioral Theory and is now called Cognitive Behavioral Therapy. *So what?* We care because "what we focus on, in part, determines how we feel."

Our brain is a part of our body, which operates dynamically and determines how we feel. The interesting thing here is that it operates fully automatically—at times. But (and it's a big but), we do choose *how* it does its job. The influence we have on how our brains work versus the automatic nature of the brain's function is an important distinction. When we don't choose our focal points, the brain will automatically do it for us. The automatic focus can be a problem for us if we are not aware of this distinction, especially when the automatic focus is of a negative nature.

There is a crazy notion that "we feel what we feel." This is not really true and thank goodness, because often I feel things that would make me act in ways that are not, shall we say, appropriate. Left to the automatic process alone, our brains can tell us to take actions people would find disturbing. One only has to look so far as parenting. There are times when my kid's actions create an automatic scenario in my brain, which seems to imply my kid might not live. Now, I say this with humor to make the point that good parents control their reactions and manage their feelings so they might come to reasonable ways to teach their children life lessons rather than harm them in any way.

We need to focus on realistic positives and not saturate our brains with negatives. It would be simplistic to say focus on the positives and not on negatives. This statement is not bad. I have said this many times. But I add the qualifier of *realistic* to draw a distinction between those who have "their heads in the clouds," or are a bit naïve about life. This is detrimental, as it will lead people to miss important facts in decision making and evaluating outcomes.

A positive focus helps us, whereas, a negative focus leads to feelings of being overwhelmed, hopeless, and powerless. When dealing with tough life issues, naturally humans seem to be tilted toward the things we are afraid of or anticipate as problems. To help ourselves, let's control what we can control, which is our focus on the matters at hand in a realistic way.

Chapter 33

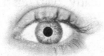

Realize change does not happen to us. It happens with us—we get to participate.

Do: Embrace change.
Don't: Resist it.

"I don't like surprises."

"Change is scary."

"I don't like not knowing."

"Climate change is fear-mongering."

"Change is intimidating."

"I don't do change."

The simple truth is: Change is inevitable. If you're like me, you might find this reality a bit unnerving. I catch myself uttering some of these statements above from time to time. Fear is a very powerful force in the human experience. When our fear becomes paralyzing, the ability to influence things or "participate" in the change happening all around us is stifled.

We can think of change as simply experiencing something new. Well now, that is a different perspective altogether, isn't it? The newness of things is refreshing. How do we feel when we have a shiny, new car or a beautiful new addition to the family? People get excited and energized around the New Year, as it represents a time for renewal. We feel ready to attack the next year with zeal. Looking at change with a different and new, if you will, perspective can go a long way to help us do what we must do anyway—embrace the change and not resist it.

And let's not forget change can be highly fruitful! I, for one, do not want to stay the same; if I did, I wouldn't grow into a better version of the person I want to be. Without change, we would be doomed to repeat things we do not want to repeat. Ever heard people exclaim, "Man, I don't want to go through that again!" Well, change is required to avoid the same pitfalls.

Rarely do concepts operate in absolutes. So, realize there are times to resist change. We do need to exercise wisdom when choosing what changes we do need to resist and which ones we need to embrace. When changes go against our morals or values, it may be a time to resist. Our country was founded on change when we seceded from the British. Talk about the need to resist! The folks up in Boston led the change with the Boston Tea Party. Britain was trying to make a change with taxes and other authoritative gestures, and we resisted! Interestingly, this resistance led us to the major change—the creation of our country and our democratic government. I believe history makes note that some of the colonists did not want to embrace this change, while others did. It was a real mixed bag. Can you see how wisdom and courage are required for these ventures to embrace change?

Mental energy is a big factor in how we operate on a daily basis. When we have negative energy around things that change, we might be doomed to repeat mistakes. However, with positive energy toward things that change, we are setting ourselves up for success.

Let's try a mental exercise. Simply change the phrases from the beginning of this section and say them out loud.

"I like surprises."

"Change is exciting."

"I like finding out about new things."

"Change is manageable."

"I need to change things up."

Some people are making a bad assumption. We assume change just happens, and we are simply left to accept what is. I don't know where or how we created this myth, but it is not true. I have come to dislike the phrase, "It is what it is." Instead, I refer people to The Serenity Prayer:

"Lord, grant me the serenity to accept the things I cannot change, the courage to change the things I can, and the wisdom to know the difference."

Some many not know this prayer goes keeps going and provides some guidance on how to proceed: "Living one moment at a time, enjoying one moment at a time; accepting hardships as a pathway to peace; taking, as Jesus did, this sinful world as it is, not as I would have it; trusting that He will make all things right if I surrender to His Will; that I may be reasonably happy in this life and supremely happy with Him forever in the next."

No matter your religious beliefs, these concepts give us excellent advice on how to participate in all that is changing around us. How we participate is up to us. We might trust in our Creator and as the prayer says, "surrender to His will." We might trust in others at times, maybe for guidance. This is why we need to strive to have good friends and faith in our life.

The simple truth is: Change is inevitable; therefore, my suggestion is to embrace change, don't fight against it, and accept the inevitable. When you accept the fact that change happens, guess what? You get to participate in the change and make a difference.

Chapter 34

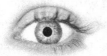

We can change our inner dialogue and cope with past hurts.

Do: Strive to understand how the
past affects you.
Don't: Discount how experiences affect you.

"Sometimes bridges need to be built before they are burned," is an idea that came from a client, whom we'll call L.M., during a session about a year before the writing of this book. She was working hard to understand the religious trauma she endured as a young child, including the sexual abuse of her sister by a church member. The family, to this day, years later, continues to operate in emotional turmoil, which has become fundamental to the way she experiences the world. For years prior to therapy, she left these events to her subconscious, trying hard to suppress it all. These suppressed memories created negative inner dialogues, which we have worked hard to expose. Through the course of her therapy, she was finally beginning to unwind the effects she has endured for a lifetime—as she was a grown adult at this point. The idea here is to connect the dots to the past so that we can then move forward in the present that we have and the future that we want including the inner dialogue that we experience. (*shared with permission, see below)

L.M. would make the point here that it is important we explore what we have experienced and find a voice to say what needs to be said. In this process, we can overcome the negative effects, change our inner dialogues, and in essence, heal. She would suggest that the bridge to those negative events can then be burned, and new ones can be created.

I loved her quote because a bridge is a connection, a tool we build for a purpose. Usually, the purpose is to get from one place to another. We must understand the connection our current mental health has to our past. We don't want to get stuck in the past, but as I've said before, we might need to glance at it. (Check out the section titled, "Focus on time: Flexible thought in the present is required to let go of regret from the past or doom of the future.")

Glancing at the past can give us a unique perspective on the present. In a military campaign, bridges are often destroyed strategically. In mental health, when we know what is behind us and what affect it has on us today, we can strategically destroy it. To do this, we take charge of our emotional selves in the present. Inner dialogue is a big part of how we feel. This is a significant part of Cognitive Behavioral Therapy, a primary type of therapy that is used in my field. Largely what we do here is challenge the inner dialogue and correct thinking errors that tend to do us harm. For instance, often people will say things like it doesn't matter what I do, things always turn bad for me.

Well, with closer examination the most telling word here is "always." This can easily be challenged because always is a word that conveys an absolute reality that is rarely a reality at all! It is not possible that things "always" turn bad, even if it seems things "often" turn bad. This process is destruction in order to reconstruct the way we want to experience the world today—destruction of our poor inner dialogue in this case.

Our experiences may not be as dramatic as sexual abuse, domestic violence, or living with an alcoholic parent. The experiences of everyday life can be essential in understanding ourselves. Misunderstandings can exist long after an initial event if they are not explored or discussed. For example, I have another active client, K.S., who recently decided to go off his anxiety medications. He had been on SSRIs (serotonin reuptake inhibitors, a type of medication that helps the use and production of the specific neurotransmitter serotonin found to affect our mood) for years. He experienced too much anxiety as a side effect and realized he functioned better on his previous medications. Through this process, he gained some insight from the reconstruction of a bridge, which he created from his past. His past included a breakup with a girlfriend that didn't understand why he was so emotional. He realized it wasn't about her at all, rather this was the last season of his life when he was unmedicated and experiencing the horrible effects of his anxiety. This was highly valuable information for him so he could destroy the angst he had about her and move on with his life, feeling free from that particular relationship.

I suggest, whether in a therapy experience, through prayer, or with a trusted friend or family member, we give credence to the life experience we've had and strive to understand how they affect us. Don't discount anything.

*I want to offer a word of thanks to the two courageous clients whom I've mentioned in this entry. I've used their stories with permission. It is to them and the many others I have had the honor and privilege of working with, developing the understanding I have today of the mental health and substance abuse issues that we face.

Conclusion

This book categorized a collection of real quotes that have been a part of many therapy sessions with many different people over the years. Far beyond the two clients I mentioned in the last entry, I harbor deep and sincere gratitude for the vulnerability people have shared with me. Sure, I learned a lot during the eight years I was in direct training to be a therapist, but there is no replacement for engaging in real conversations with real people. It's how I have learned all I know about emotion management.

I have learned that human beings are so dynamic and individualized we cannot categorize them with an easy diagnosis or a simple label. This is something people fear, and rightfully so. I have also learned we cannot compartmentalize any single emotion, feeling, or situation. We do not operate in a vacuum. We *can* understand human patterns, though, including our own patterns and grow from them. This is, in part, what this project is intended to accomplish in your journey.

I would like to instill a little hope in emotion management for people, because there is great hope, even when we may feel we are drowning in our most desperate times.

An example of one of these desperate times is when people feel suicidal. Unfortunately, there is a bit of a myth about suicide. Many people don't understand how someone can get to the point of desperation where they think taking his or her life is the only answer. There is an inaccurate belief that the individual knows a combination of their "truth": the pain that he feels and the act of having tried everything he knows to feel better. He knows he feels bad—really bad—and he has tried "everything" he knows to do to feel better. The combination, in thought, is that he knows he cannot continue to live feeling as bad as he does, and since he's tried "everything," he feels as though he has only one option left—to end his life.

The truth, as best as I can speak of it, is there is never an end to the combinations of skills one can use to cope with this thing called life. That is the simple truth, as I see it. Now mind you, we don't have to get to this depth to feel frustrated with emotions. If you feel like you've stumbled into a bad emotional place, I hope this project gives you confidence and skills, in isolation or in combination with each other, to encourage you that you can cope with whatever life is throwing at you!

This has been an exciting little journey for me. Here is my final pledge: I am not done. There is more to come. I chose to start with "The Self," because it is primary. Self is the priority in emotion management; however, we all know that we deal with other people, and I have a lot of ideas about what can be helpful in different relational arenas. I have more projects "cooked up in my head," that I want to share. The areas I focus on in therapy with men, women, elderly, and children include marriage, parenting, and friendships with others. So until we meet again through text or other media, I hope you find joy in referring to these ideas, and grow in your journey. May you be emotionally well!

Endnotes

The Self

1   Chapman, Gary. *The Five Love Languages*. Chicago: Northfield Publishing (a division of Moody Publishers), 2015, reprint.

Chapter 1

2   Franklin D. Roosevelt, Inaugural Address, March 4, 1933, as published in Samuel Rosenman, ed., *The Public Papers of Franklin D. Roosevelt, Volume Two: The Year of Crisis, 1933* (New York: Random House, 1938), 11–16.

Chapter 6

3   Peale, Norman Vincent. *The Power of Positive Thinking*. Lexington: Touchstone Publishing Company, 2003, reprint.

Chapter 16

4   **"Second marriages are sixty-seven percent..."** Banschick M.D., Mark. "The High Failure Rate of Second and Third Marriages." *Psychology Today*. Sussex Publishers, LLC, 06 Feb 2012. Accessed 04 Dec 2019, https://www.psychologytoday.com/us/blog/the-intelligent-

divorce/201202/the-high-failure-rate-second-and-third-marriages.

Chapter 17

5 **"...children have the ability to model behavior."** Rymanowicz, Kylie. "Monkey See, Monkey Do: Model Behavior in Early Childhood." *Michigan State University Extension*. Michigan State University, 30 March 2015. Accessed 04 Dec 2019, https://www.canr.msu.edu/news/monkey_see_monkey_do_model_behavior_in_early_childhood.

Chapter 29

6 **"It is better to teach..."** Ritchie, Isabella Thackeray. *Mrs. Dymond*. Stroud, Gloucestershire, United Kingdom: Sutton Publishing Ltd, 1999, reprint. (Original 1885).

Chapter 33

7 Niebuhr, Reinhold. "The Serenity Prayer," as part of his sermon at Heath Evangelical Union Church in Massachusetts, 1934.

About the Author

Chris Gazdik has been a practicing mental health and substance abuse counselor for over twenty years. He is co-founder of the Psychological Services of Charlotte and founder of Metrolina Psychotherapy Associates. Chris is also the founder of a fun and  interesting podcast called *Through a Therapist's Eyes*.

Chris earned his bachelor's degree (BSW) and a Master's degree of Social Work (MSW) from West Virginia University, where -he graduated with honors (Magna cum Laude). Being a proud mountaineer from the state of West Virginia, his work in the mental health and substance abuse field as a therapist and public speaker has taken many forms. He has been a DUI class instructor, crisis intervention specialist, family support worker, and has practiced in mental health centers and direct therapy practice agencies. He has also worked with the School of Social Work at the University of North Carolina Charlotte as a field liaison and been a preceptor with Gardner-Webb University's Physician Assistant's program.

For more information, visit
www.throughatherapistseyes.com.

CPSIA information can be obtained
at www.ICGtesting.com
Printed in the USA
JSHW032056230221
12017JS00002B/119